THE BATTLE OF
TASSAFARONGA

THE BATTLE OF
TASSAFARONGA

Russell Sydnor Crenshaw Jr.

NAVAL INSTITUTE PRESS
Annapolis, Maryland

Naval Institute Press
291 Wood Road
Annapolis, MD 21402

This book has been brought to publication with the generous assistance of
Marguerite and Gerry Lenfest.

First Naval Institute Press paperback edition published 2010.

Library of Congress Cataloging-in-Publication Data
Crenshaw, Russell Sydnor, 1920–
  The Battle of Tassafaronga / Russell Sydnor Crenshaw Jr.
      p. cm.
  Includes index.
  Originally published: Baltimore, Md. : Nautical & Aviation Pub. Co., c1995.
  ISBN 978-1-59114-146-4 (alk. paper)
  1. Tassafaronga, Battle of, Solomon Islands, 1942. 2. World War, 1939–1945—Naval
operations, American. I. Title.
  D774.T38C74 2010
  940.54'265933—dc22

                                                        2010011646

Printed in the United States of America on acid-free paper

14 13 12 11 10   9 8 7 6 5 4 3 2
First printing

Published in association with the Destroyer History Foundation, www.destroyerhistory.org
David W. McComb, President

∽ Contents ∽

∽ *Illustrations* ∽

$\_\sim$ *Foreword* $\sim\_$

The Battle of Tassafaronga,[*] the last of the "Battles of Savo Island" in the Guadalcanal campaign of World War II, was little noted on the pages of history, yet it was one of the most significant. It marked the defeat of the Japanese thrust into the Solomon Islands and convinced the Japanese high command that they must start the retreat that eventually led to the surrender in Tokyo Bay. In that sense, it was as significant as the Battle of Midway.

For the United States Navy, the battle was a horrible embarrassment, the more quickly forgotten, the better: one heavy cruiser sunk and three heavy cruisers heavily damaged in exchange for uncertain losses by the enemy. Like most of the previous engagements in these troubled waters it was difficult to determine just what had happened. The reports by observers did not correspond with the known facts. It was difficult to explain how the damage to our ships had occurred. There was an aura of mystery about the whole affair.

The author was the gunnery officer of the USS *Maury*, DD-401, third ship in the van of the American force. Although he felt sure his ship and the other three destroyers had done their jobs as well as any ships could under the circumstances, he was never satisfied that he really knew what had happened on the night of the 30th of November 1942. While doing some research in the Operational Archives of the U.S. Naval Historical Center at the Washington Navy Yard, he came across clues that led him to delve more deeply. With enough information to reconstruct the battle, he gradually came to realize what had happened. He discovered that this forgotten battle was not just a stepping-stone in a long and difficult campaign, it was a crucible in which the very nature of the U.S. Navy and its weapons was tested. It was a miniature of what might have been, under other circumstances, a truly devastating defeat.

---

[*]   Tasivarongo: *tasi* "sea" + *varongo* "quiet"

—⁓ *Acknowledgments* ⁓—

S o much of this work has been drawn from other sources that it is impractical to annotate the entire text and burden the pages with footnotes. The author has therefore chosen to give credit for entire areas as follows:

For the general history of the Solomon Islands campaign and all other specific battles, except the Battle of Tassafaronga, Samuel Eliot Morison's *History of the United States Naval Operations in World War II,* published by Little, Brown and Company, was the principal source. For additional specific information about destroyers (other than the *Maury* in other battles), he relied on Theodore Roscoe's *Destroyer Operations in World War II,* published by the United States Naval Institute.

The key to the Japanese side of the battle was found in *The Japanese Navy in World War II* by Paul Dull, published by the U.S. Naval Institute, and in Chapter 5 of *The Struggle for Guadalcanal,* by Rear Admiral Raizo Tanaka, Imperial Japanese Navy.

Admiral Tanaka commanded most of the resupply efforts made by the Japanese during the Guadalcanal campaign and was in command of the Japanese force at Tassafaronga. Chapter VII, "The Tokyo Express," is an abbreviation of Admiral Tanaka's fascinating account of his long struggle, and Chapter VIII, "The Other Side," includes his observations and recollections during the battle wherever his name is mentioned.

For all official documents, particularly those mentioned in the following paragraphs, the U.S. Naval Historical Center at the Washington Navy Yard is the source and the author is indebted to its efficient and helpful staff.

The history of the Long Lance torpedo and its effect on Japanese naval planning reported in Chapter VI is drawn in part from Admiral Tanaka's article and in part from reports of interviews of Japanese officers by the members of the U.S. Strategic Bombing Survey (Pacific) following the hostilities. The technical details and performance of the Japanese Type 93 torpedo were found in the report of the U.S. Naval Technical Mission to Japan's report on Japanese Torpedoes and Tubes.

In Chapter IX, "The Torpedo Problem," the history of the U.S. Navy's torpedo program and the steps eventually taken to uncover and correct torpedo deficiencies is based on Buford Rowland and William B. Boyd's *Bureau of Ordnance in World War II,* published by the U.S. Government Printing Office in 1953. The letter by Dr. Albert Einstein was shown to the author by Captain R. C. Gillette, who was preparing the reference library for the new Naval Submarine Museum at Keyport, Washington.

The actions and opinions of the American commanders involved are drawn from the following Action Reports, originally classified as secret:

Commander Task Force Sixty Seven Serial 06 of December 9, 1942. Rear Admiral C. H. Wright's official "Report on Action off Cape Esperance, Night of November 30, 1942."

Commander South Pacific Area and South Pacific Force Serial 00411 of February 20, 1943. Admiral W. F. Halsey's "First Endorsement" to Admiral Wright's report.

Commander in Chief, U.S. Pacific Fleet Serial 00546 of February 15, 1943. Admiral C. W. Nimitz's report to Commander in Chief, U.S. Fleet, Admiral E. J. King.

Commander Task Unit Sixty-Seven Point Two Point Three Serial 042 of December 6, 1942. Rear Admiral M. S. Tisdale's report to Admiral Wright.

Commanding Officer, USS *Fletcher,* DD-445, Action Report Serial (s)-3 of December 3, 1942.

Commanding Officer, USS *Perkins,* DD-377, Action Report, Serial 01854 of December 1, 1942.

Commanding Officer, USS *Maury,* DD-401, Action Report, Serial 026 of December 3, 1942.

Commanding Officer, USS *Drayton,* DD-366, Action Report, Serial 057 of December 3, 1942.

Commanding Officer, USS *Minneapolis,* CA-36, Action Report, Serial 0247 of 6 December, 1942.

Commanding Officer, USS *New Orleans,* CA-32, Action Report, Serial 071 of December 4, 1942.

Commanding Officer, USS *Pensacola,* CA-24, Action Report, Serial 0178 of December 4, 1942.

Commanding Officer, USS *Honolulu,* CL-48, Action Report, Serial 0142 of December 4, 1942.

Commanding Officer, USS *Northampton,* CA-26, Action Report, without serial number, of December 5, 1942.

Commanding Officer, USS *Lamson,* DD-367, Action Report, Serial 00242 of December 3, 1942.

Commanding Officer, USS *Lardner,* DD-487, Action Report, without serial number, of December 8, 1942.

In addition to the sources mentioned above, a full translation of the Japanese report on the Battle of Tassafaronga on 30 November 1942, identified as ATIS Document 16086, was obtained from the Historical Center. This document was used as the basis for all of the Japanese actions and times during the engagement. The Japanese diagram of the battle, although not to scale or precisely drawn, was used as the basis for the maneuvers of the individual Japanese ships.

The Washington Document Center documents, WDC 161711 and WDC 160702, the "Records and Operations of the Japanese 2nd Destroyer Squadron," were used to verify the recollections of Admiral Tanaka.

For the characteristics of the Japanese destroyers, Anthony J. Watts' excellent *Japanese Warships of World War II,* published by Doubleday & Company, Inc., was used as the reference.

The photographs in this work were obtained from the U.S. Naval Institute, the National Archives, or the National Institute for Defense Studies, Tokyo, Japan, as indicated in the captions. The calculation of the time of moonrise on the night of the battle was supplied by the U.S. Naval Observatory.

For Chapters X, XI, and XII, the author depended on his own experience in destroyers and cruisers as well as his years in the research and development community, working on the design and production of naval weapons and the control systems associated with them.

THE BATTLE OF

TASSAFARONGA

I

PROLOG

Carleton Wright settled back in his comfortable swivel chair on the flag bridge of the USS *Minneapolis* and continued to stare forward over her two massive turrets with their triple 8-inch guns, studying the horizon ahead. His steward, feet spread against the gentle roll of the ship, skillfully poured a hot stream of coffee into the single cup centered on the carefully folded white linen napkin on the silver tray balanced in his left hand. The graceful cup and its matching saucer were trimmed in gold and bore the two stars of a Rear Admiral. Wright had been commander of Cruiser Division Six for several months and had ridden his flagship through the carrier battles since the invasion of the Solomon Islands with the *Saratoga* Task Force, but just the day before yesterday he had assumed the duties of Commander Task Force Sixty-Seven, and he was now on his way to meet the Japanese at Savo Island. All hands knew the admiral had much on his mind, so the steward placed the tray on the shelf by the admiral's hand and quietly disappeared below.

Wright stared ahead across the oil-blue water to tufts of clouds that hung over San Cristobal, the first of the Solomons and the entrance to Indispensable Straits, but he wasn't seeing anything; his mind was on the coming operation. Admiral Halsey had given him all the ships available: four heavy cruisers, one big light cruiser, and the only four destroyers he could find. It wasn't the perfect force, but those 8-inch and 6-inch guns had plenty of punch.

In the previous battles off Guadalcanal his predecessors had been badly mauled by the Japanese, so he was going to be sure he didn't repeat their mistakes.

He had served in the four piper *Jarvis* in the Queenstown Command under Commodore Taussig in the First World War, worked his way up the ladder to command a destroyer, later a division, and just before the war had commanded the heavy cruiser *Augusta,* Flagship of the Asiatic Fleet. Starting from an ordnance postgraduate course immediately after World War I, he had served in ordnance billets both ashore and at sea, and during his last tour ashore had commanded the Navy Mine Depot at Yorktown. For the last half year he had commanded Cruiser Division Six, the best in the Pacific Fleet. If there was anyone prepared to fight cruisers and destroyers, it should be him.

Though he had relieved Rear Admiral Tommy Kinkaid as commander of Task Force Sixty-Seven only two days before, he had been a flag officer in the forward area since the invasion of the Solomons on 7 August. Flag officers had codes to break many messages not cleared for release to lower commands—they had the "need to know"—so Wright had read every report or comment on the previous battles up to the minute. It was now the 30th of November 1942.

The first battle at Savo Island, on the night of 8–9 August, a scarce 42 hours after the invasion, had been an unbelievable fiasco. His own CruDiv 6 had been with the *Saratoga* Task Force southeast of the Solomons at the time, but four American and three Australian cruisers with about a dozen destroyers were in the sound between Tulagi and Guadalcanal, guarding the transports and cargo ships. They were divided into three groups, one each guarding the entrances to the sound to the north and south of Savo, and a small group watching the eastern entrances. Rear Admiral Kelly Turner, Commander of the Amphibious Force, was in overall command and Rear Admiral Crutchley, RN, in HMAS *Australia,* had command of all of the cruisers and destroyers. Admiral Turner had called Admiral Crutchley to a late night conference aboard his flagship, transport *Mc-Cawley,* lying-to off Lunga Point, where the Marines had landed on Guadalcanal Island.

The crews of the allied ships, at battle stations for most of the preceding days, were exhausted from the stresses of the invasion. The two western groups were patrolling sleepily at low speed in their areas, depending on destroyers *Blue* and *Ralph Talbot,* posted as pickets to the west, to warn them if any enemy ships approached.

A bit after midnight a couple of strange aircraft were sighted and reported by the pickets and even one of the northern cruisers, but nothing was made of it. Although there was apparently some attempt at warning by the pickets, a Japanese force suddenly appeared between Savo and Cape Esperance, the northwestern tip of Guadalcanal, and proceeded to shoot up the southern group. Destroyer *Patterson* on the port bow of the cruiser column shouted warning and opened fire, but HMAS *Canberra,* leading the two cruisers, began taking hits from Japanese shells before she could react—then two Japanese torpedoes blasted into her starboard side. Destroyer *Bagley,* on the starboard bow, spun around and got off a spread of eight torpedoes, but the Japanese column was already speeding away.

Heavy cruiser *Chicago,* following in the wake of *Canberra,* was still trying to figure out what was happening when part of her bow was blown off by a Japanese torpedo. Stunned and confused, she fired star shells into the night to find her enemy—the fuzes weren't set, so they were duds. A searchlight flashed ahead—she fired 25 rounds at it before it went out. She tried her own searchlight. Seeing nothing, she closed its shutter and staggered on past the blazing *Canberra,* never finding her adversary and, unbelievably, never transmitting any alarm or warning!

It was a hazy night with occasional showers, so when Japanese floatplanes dropped brilliant flares over Lunga Point, all eyes turned in that direction while the Japanese column turned to the north. Heavy cruisers *Vincennes, Quincy,* and *Astoria,* with destroyers *Wilson* and *Helm* screening ahead, were plodding around a square to the northeast of Savo at 10 knots and had just made a column movement to the northwest when the Japanese force opened fire. It was incredible that these ships had not heard the radio transmissions of the pickets or noticed the flashes of gunfire to the south, but they were not even at general quarters.

Astoria, last ship in column, was the first to be engaged. Her bridge watch was still pondering the meaning of the flares over Lunga when her gunnery officer, up checking his men, sighted the approaching Japanese column, sounded the general alarm, and ordered the sparsely manned turrets to commence firing. The startled captain arrived on the bridge as the second salvo blasted out, ordered cease-fire, and demanded to know what was going on. By the time the captain was convinced that his gun boss was right and permitted fire to be resumed, the Japanese cruisers found the range and 8-inch shells crashed into *Astoria*'s superstructure. The planes on the catapults caught fire and topsides turned into a raging inferno. She kept firing, but her hull was holed. Soon she lost power and steering control, then drifted out of the battle. Her crew fought the fires and flooding desperately, but she was deeply wounded and couldn't be saved. It was a long battle against continual fires and progressive flooding. She finally went under just after noon the next day.

Quincy, next in column, took an even more intense beating and quickly became a flaming torch. In addition to the pounding of 8-inch shells from two directions, she took a torpedo amidships, her number two turret exploded, and her bridge was wiped out, mortally wounding her captain. She rolled over and sank in 40 minutes.

Vincennes, whose captain commanded the northern group, had a nearly identical experience. Doubt on the bridge, quick heavy hits torching off planes and aviation gas, two torpedoes amidships within five minutes, another a bit later, towering flames from bow to stern, all guns and turrets knocked out, she slowly rolled over on her side and was gone within an hour.

Radar had failed to warn, voice radio messages didn't get through, lookouts and control officers were blinded by the flares, fires, and gun flashes, and the enemy just steamed through and shot up everything in sight. It was a good thing that the Japanese continued to the northwest into the black of the night because the transports near Tulagi and Lunga Point would have made sweet pickings.

To avoid the hazards of aircraft and aviation gasoline, Wright had already left half of the cruiser's planes in Espiritu and had flown off the remainder to Tulagi, to be clear of the ships and be ready for observation and illumination when requested during the night. He had also ordered all ships in his force to dispose of any inflammables not in fireproof stowage.

The second battle of Savo Island in the middle of October had been a good deal better, but there was still a lot of room for improvement. Rear Admiral Norman Scott, a class ahead of Wright at the Naval Academy, had his ships under tight control and had a positive plan of action. Flying his flag in the heavy cruiser *San Francisco* followed by the older *Salt Lake City* plus two of the fast-firing 6-inch-gun light cruisers, *Boise* and *Helena,* he had plenty of firepower, and he had five of the new 1,600-ton destroyers under command of their own commodore, Captain R. G. Tobin, ComDesRon 12.

Ever since the first battle of Savo Island, the Japanese had been trying to reinforce their troops on Guadalcanal and particularly to knock out Henderson Field, sitting like an unsinkable aircraft carrier in the midst of the battle zone. Although a major Japanese effort had been turned back in late August, culminating in the carrier battle off Stewart Island,[1] Henderson Field had been bombarded frequently both from the air and from the sea. Scott was sent up from Espiritu

---

1 Battle of the Eastern Solomons

to block a new attempt to cripple the airfield. Reconnaissance and intelligence was so good that a half hour before midnight on the 11th of October, Scott was able to intercept the leading Japanese force about 15 miles to the west of Savo Island.

Radar contact was made to the northwest at 27,000 yards and it was quickly apparent that the American column was crossing ahead of the Japanese column—capping the enemy's tee. To continue in this most desirable of positions, Scott ordered a countermarch, which called for his cruisers to reverse course in a column movement turning toward the enemy and required the three lead destroyers to move up the engaged side and reposition themselves ahead of the flagship. The maneuver was ordered too late. The battle broke out when the closest enemy ship reached 5,000 yards from the American cruisers with the three lead destroyers caught in the middle.

Scott's cruisers concentrated on the lead ship of three Japanese heavy cruisers, immediately scoring hits. Fearing his cruisers were firing into his own destroyers, however, and after only a minute of fire, Scott ordered, "Cease fire." But the battle was joined and his order was only partially effective.

Tobin's flagship *Farenholt,* racing to her position ahead, was hit from both sides. *Duncan,* next in column, sighted the enemy visually while still in her turn and, remembering Scott's standing order to engage when in sight, rang up 30 knots and charged directly at the enemy cruisers, guns blazing. She quickly found herself between the lead Japanese cruiser and a flank destroyer. Careening left to keep her guns bearing and to fire her torpedoes, she was pummeled from all sides. A shell exploded in her fireroom and began to slow her down, her gun director and forward stack were both shot away, ready service ammunition blew up and set her afire, and then a salvo from the friendly side wiped her out topside. Crippled and burning fiercely, she circled to the north out of the battle.

Laffey, last of the van destroyers, perceiving the ghastly situation, backed emergency and turned hard left to fall in astern of the cruisers. Luckily the Japanese were caught unprepared and also were not sure who was friend or foe.

After several minutes of radio queries to Commodore Tobin to make sure where his destroyers were, Scott ordered, "Resume fire." By this time the Japanese had reversed course to the northwest, so Scott led his column right to parallel the enemy. *San Francisco* sighted a shadow close aboard, and snapped open her searchlight shutters to reveal a Japanese destroyer. Her guns led the other ships in blasting it to oblivion. A bit later *Boise* tried her searchlight and was nearly blown out of the water in return. Burning from bow to stern, with most of her guns silenced, *Boise* fell out of the column and headed south to retire.

After half an hour of heavy fighting, a Japanese cruiser and a Japanese destroyer definitely had been sunk and the remaining enemy ships were scurrying away at top speed, so Scott broke off the engagement to cover *Boise* and *Farenholt*. He also wanted to be ready should another Japanese force appear out of the night. *Duncan* was a blazing inferno and had to be abandoned, sinking about noon the following day. *Boise* had to be sent back to the States to be rebuilt. *Salt Lake City* received such heavy damage that she had to return to Pearl Harbor for repairs.

This second battle of Savo Island[2] was certainly better than the first, with heavy damage on both sides. Although initial reports, particularly in the stateside press, painted an encouraging picture, with *Boise* in an heroic role, two U.S. cruisers and two destroyers knocked out of action in exchange for one cruiser and one destroyer definitely sunk and unknown, but hopefully heavy, damage to two more cruisers. Of vital importance to the battle on Guadalcanal, however, another Japanese force, following the group that Scott had fought, had succeeded in landing a large contingent of troops and material near Koli Point and got away without being engaged.

Wright could not imagine what had led Scott to order such a complicated countermarch in the middle of the night with the enemy closing in. A simple course reversal by simultaneous turn would have accomplished the same objective and been completed in less than three minutes. It was also dramatically clear that using a searchlight in a night action was an invitation to suicide. He did not have a chance to talk to Scott—Norman did not live long enough.

Then Wright thought about the three days of bloody struggle around Savo two weeks ago on the 13th through 15th of November. It was another multi-headed push by the whole Japanese fleet, just like the one turned back in October, but this time it coincided with an armed reinforcement of our own troops. The first contingent of three AKAs, protected by Admiral Scott in *Atlanta* and four destroyers, arrived at Lunga Point on the 11th and began discharging their heavy equipment. At dawn on the 12th Kelly Turner in *McCawley* arrived with a total of four heavily loaded transports escorted by Rear Admiral Dan Callaghan's force of five cruisers and eight destroyers. Task Force Sixteen under Tommy Kinkaid in *Enterprise* was coming up from Nouméa to back up the landings, but

---

2   Battle of Cape Esperance

the "Big E" had to steam slowly to permit the repair work of her bomb damage at Santa Cruz[3] to continue. As a consequence, Rear Admiral Willis A. Lee, with battleships *Washington* and *South Dakota* and with four destroyers, had been sent ahead to stand by.

There were many indications that the Japanese weren't going to let our reinforcement go unopposed. Scott's force had been sighted and tailed by a long-range search plane on the 10th and they'd hardly started unloading on the 11th when the first Japanese dive-bombers arrived. With plenty of warning, Scott had gotten his ships underway and no ship was actually hit, but *Zeilin,* an attack cargo ship, suffered underwater hull damage from a near miss and had to be sent south, taking half her cargo with her. In the afternoon, a high-flying formation of Japanese twin-engine "Bettys" rained bombs on Henderson Field.

On the afternoon of the 12th the entire combined amphibious force had to interrupt unloading to face a maximum-effort Japanese raid using all types of aircraft. Fighters from Henderson Field hit the high-level and dive bombers well to the west of Savo and knocked down many before they got in, but two dozen Bettys armed with torpedoes skimmed in just above the waves to get at the fat amphibians. Turner handled his force smartly and avoided all of the torpedoes while the blazing AA fire from his ships and friendly fighters shot down almost all of the Bettys. It wasn't without cost however. Callaghan's flagship, *San Francisco,* was hit in the after superstructure by a dying Betty, knocking out her after AA control station and wounding 50 men, and destroyer *Buchanan* was so badly damaged by friendly fire that she had to be sent out of the battle area.

Meanwhile, long-range reconnaissance planes and coastwatchers were reporting a multitude of Japanese forces heading for Guadalcanal. Two battleships accompanied by a cruiser and six destroyers were sighted 300 miles to the north. Five destroyers were found at 200 miles to the north-northwest. Two carriers with two destroyers were spotted 265 miles to the west and a heavy concentration of shipping was reported in the Buin-Shortland area, only 280 miles to the northwest as the crow flies. Feeling sure an attack was imminent, Turner withdrew his amphibious force to the relative safety of Indispensable Straits to the east. As soon as they were safely through Lengo Channel, he sent Callaghan back with all of his cruisers and eight destroyers to meet the enemy. By nightfall it was evident that the Japanese battleships, soon to be identified as *Hiei* and *Kirishima,*

---

3   Battle of the Santa Cruz Islands, 26 October 1942

accompanied by a dozen destroyers and a light cruiser, were roaring south to neutralize Henderson Field.

Callaghan, in *San Francisco,* deployed his force in one long column with Commander T. M. Stokes, ComDesDiv 10, in *Cushing,* leading *Laffey, Sterett,* and *O'Bannon* as the van destroyers, followed by his cruisers in the order of *Atlanta, San Francisco, Portland, Helena,* and *Juneau.* Scott was in *Atlanta* as second in command, Callaghan being a year senior to him. The rear was brought up by Captain Tobin, ComDesRon 12, now in *Aaron Ward,* followed by *Barton, Monssen,* and *Fletcher.* Shortly after 0100 on Friday the 13th, Callaghan's long column passed a mile north of Lunga Point heading west.

First contact was made at 0124 by *Helena's* excellent SG radar—two contacts to the northwest, one at 27,000 yards and the other at 32,000 yards— extraordinary ranges. Three minutes later Callaghan ordered his column right to 310° T to head directly at the contacts. For ten minutes he held this course, asking repeatedly for target information from *Helena* and *O'Bannon,* because *San Francisco* didn't have a good surface search radar, but he issued no tactical orders or battle instructions as the range to the enemy plunged. At 0137, with the closest enemy contact less than 10,000 yards away, he finally ordered his column to a course of due north and increased speed to 20 knots. The tactical voice radio circuit, the TBS, was clogged with multiple target reports, ranges, and bearings, but no commands.

At 0141 *Cushing,* at the head of the 13-ship column, now bent in the middle because half of the ships had not yet reached the point at which to turn north, sighted two Japanese destroyers crossing ahead from port to starboard. Her captain, Lieutenant Commander Edward N. Parker, sounded the alarm and came left 45° to unmask her batteries. *Laffey,* next astern, followed her lead, but *Sterett* and *O'Bannon* continued due north. *Atlanta,* just completing her turn and not knowing what was transpiring ahead, sheered out of the column to the left. Callaghan, observing this unexpected maneuver, asked *Atlanta* what she was doing. Captain Samuel P. Jenkins replied, "Avoiding our own destroyers," and swung back to parallel the column. Meanwhile, Commodore Stokes, in *Cushing,* watching the enemy ships slip by, asked permission to fire torpedoes; Callaghan granted permission, but by the time it was received, the targets had disappeared in the gloom. The clock ticked on. Confusion and doubt reigned on the American bridges.

Finally at 0145 Callaghan ordered, "Stand by to open fire." This was enough for Stokes. *Cushing* opened fire to starboard at a light cruiser close aboard. She was quickly hit by return fire at the point-blank range, lost power, and began to slow. A huge Japanese battleship appeared to port, *Cushing* came slowly right with what speed remained and fired six torpedoes at the looming menace, three of which her crew thought had hit. As the battleship, later identified as *Hiei,* charged by, *Cushing* was caught in the beam of a searchlight, ripped apart by a rain of shells and set afire from stem to stern.

Laffey continued past *Cushing,* then came back to the formation course of north only to find that she was on a collision course with the huge battlewagon, a thousand yards to port. She fired two fish, crossed the enemy's bow, but had to use hard left rudder to get her stern by, and raked the length of the Japanese ship with every gun and machine gun that would bear. She had hardly passed clear when she was struck by two 14-inch salvoes, then hit by a torpedo in her stern. Engines demolished, afire topsides and flooding rapidly aft, her captain, Lieutenant Commander William E. Hank, ordered, "Abandon ship." The men got into the water in good order, but when she actually sank about a quarter of an hour later, her depth charges went off, killing most of the survivors.

Sterett had continued on course 000° T in accordance with Callaghan's last order, despite *Cushing* and *Laffey's* turn to the left. *O'Bannon* followed in her wake. After the firefight had broken out at the head of the column, Callaghan ordered, "Odd ships commence fire to starboard, even ships to port." *Sterett's* captain, Commander Jesse G. Coward, obediently opened up to starboard under full radar control on the two destroyers that had passed ahead and disappeared. After a few salvoes, *Sterett* was struck aft by Japanese shells from port, momentarily knocking out her steering control, and another shell struck her mast knocking out her radar. She then spotted the charging *Hiei* to port and, steering with her engines, got off four torpedoes at an ideal range of about 2,000 yards, but observed no hits as the big ship passed astern.

O'Bannon, Commander Edwin R. Wilkinson commanding, with one of only three SG radars in the whole American column, had an excellent picture of the whole scene and was carefully selecting the best target. As she sheered left to avoid the wounded *Sterett,* she opened fire at the thundering *Hiei* at a range of only 1,200 yards and fired two torpedoes, which were seen to pass right under the battlewagon, but there was no explosion. She was pouring everything she had into the battleship as she passed down her side on an opposite course when an unbelievable order, "Cease firing own ships," came in over the TBS. Captain Wilkinson checked fire.

At 0150 a Japanese searchlight caught *Atlanta*, illuminating her high stepped superstructure like daylight. She opened fire with her multiple 5-inch mounts at shadowy targets both to starboard and to port. The Japanese searchlight was quickly extinguished, but many other enemy ships concentrated their fire on her and in a moment *Atlanta* was deluged with shells, killing Admiral Scott and most of his staff. Some of the shells hitting *Atlanta* may have come from American muzzles, thus prompting Callaghan's order. In any case, *Atlanta* was ripped to pieces topside, took at least one Japanese torpedo amidships, slowed to a stop and drifted out of the action, a flaming wreck.

San Francisco opened fire on an enemy ship at short range on her starboard beam, got off seven 8-inch salvoes, but was soon illuminated by a searchlight further aft. She shifted to the source of the searchlight and had set the ship afire when a Japanese battleship on her starboard bow began to pummel her with 14-inch shells. It was at this time that Callaghan's "Cease firing own ships" interrupted her fighting. She was almost immediately the simultaneous target of the two ships to starboard and a Japanese destroyer to port. Her superstructure was blasted to a shambles, killing Admiral Callaghan and his staff as well as her captain, Cassin Young, and almost everyone on the bridge. With topsides flaming, she lost engine and steering control and slowed to a crawl.

Portland, astern of the flagship, engaged the enemy targets to starboard with steady salvoes from her 8-inch turrets. Captain Laurance T. DuBose could not believe he had heard Callaghan's strange order correctly and asked, "What's the dope?" Receiving a reply that Callaghan had meant it, he checked fire briefly, but opened again as soon as he found a new target he was sure was enemy. *Portland* had hardly resumed fire when she caught a Japanese torpedo aft, ripping out her hull plates into a fixed rudder to starboard and forcing her into an involuntary turn to the right. As she completed the first circle, she got off a telling salvo at one of the Japanese battleships, but continued to circle helplessly.

Helena, Captain Gilbert C. Hoover commanding, joined the fray as the ships ahead opened fire and lashed out at a searchlight to port. As the Japanese battleships passed through the column ahead, leaving *Cushing, Laffey, Atlanta,* and *San Francisco* as flaming obstacles, Captain Hoover threaded his way gingerly through the turmoil. His 6-inch turrets punished a Japanese ship that was pummeling the flagship from port while his 5-inch and 40-mm batteries raked two different targets to starboard. Despite the intensity of the battle, *Helena* received only minor damage in her superstructure.

Not so for *Juneau*. Captain Lyman K. Swenson opened fire with his multiple 5-inch mounts whenever a searchlight was spotted, but he had difficulty finding any other targets. A bit after he ordered, "Check fire," following Callaghan's order, a Japanese torpedo caught *Juneau* amidships and knocked her completely out of action. She lost all power and lay dead in the water.

Aaron Ward, Tobin's flagship, had no SG and had to search carefully for a target in the evolving confusion ahead. She finally focused on a target 7,000 yards on her starboard bow, which Captain Orville F. Gregor felt sure was enemy, and got off ten salvoes of 5-inch before the line of fire was fouled by friendly cruisers. *Portland* was circling to starboard, *Juneau* was blasted, and unexpectedly, *San Francisco* hove into sight. Gregor had to back to keep from ramming a ship ahead, probably *Helena*. As *Aaron Ward* came clear of the pileup, she engaged a ship to starboard that had flashed strange recognition lights and continued her fire until the ship appeared to blow up and sink. During the exchange, she was hit in her gun director and had to shift her 5-inch to local control.

Barton joined the battle with the ships ahead and even got off four torpedoes at a Japanese ship to port. Her captain, Lieutenant Commander Douglas H. Fox, backed "emergency" to avoid colliding with *Aaron Ward* when she backed and, while almost dead in the water, caught two torpedoes amidships, broke in two and sank, taking most of her crew with her.

Monssen had lost her fire control radar during the air attacks in the afternoon, so she was even more blind than the others. She finally sighted a Japanese battleship on her starboard bow and fired a spread of five torpedoes at it. She next spotted another target on her starboard beam and let fly her last five torpedoes. She then found targets and opened fire to port, even strafing a Japanese destroyer with 20-mm as it raced past at less than 1,000 yards. Star shells began to illuminate her, so her skipper, Lieutenant Commander Charles E. McCombs, ordered her fighting lights turned on. This brought searchlights from two directions and a deluge of shells. Thirty-seven hits reduced her to a burning hulk.

Fletcher, last of the 13-ship column and the leader of the class of new 2,100-ton destroyers, with Commander William M. Cole in command, was equipped with an SG radar and her crew knew how to use it. She first opened fire at 5,500 yards on the ship to port that was illuminating *Atlanta*. Seeing other ships were adequately taking care of that Jap, Cole shifted his fire to a more distant target and set it afire. Callaghan's cease-fire order caused him to check fire, but he soon opened again on a Japanese ship at even longer range to port. He could see on his SG PPI scope that the column had disintegrated, and when *Barton* blew up and *Monssen* was ignited, Cole decided to get clear. He cranked on 35 knots and came left to parallel the coast of Guadalcanal and get around the flank of the enemy. As the firing began to recede, he selected the biggest radar blip he could find, a Japanese on an easterly course, still firing at ships to the north, and after tracking the target carefully for several minutes, fired a full salvo of ten torpedoes for a torpedo run of 7,000 yards. He then headed east toward Sealark Channel to await further orders, there having been no evidence of command since Callaghan's strange order to cease fire.

Dawn found Captain Hoover in *Helena,* with *Fletcher* and *O'Bannon* escorting the damaged *San Francisco, Juneau,* and *Sterett* down Indispensable Straits to the southeast. *Portland* still circled despite numerous measures to compensate for her unwanted "rudder," *Atlanta* was anchored in deep water off Lunga Point, *Cushing* and *Monssen* were dead in the water and still burning, and *Aaron Ward,* which had caught nine shell hits at the tail end of the battle, had a flooded engine room and floated helplessly, deep in the water halfway to Tulagi.

A few salvoes from *Portland* sent the abandoned hulk of the Japanese destroyer *Yudachi* to the bottom. The battered Japanese battleship *Hiei,* having lost her steering gear and most of her firepower from innumerable shell hits, both large and small, was creeping along just north of Savo Island, but soon the Marine planes from Henderson Field, augmented by SBDs and TBFs sent up from the approaching *Enterprise,* started working her over. She was abandoned and sank before the end of the day. *Aaron Ward* was towed to the relative safety of Tulagi. *Atlanta,* hopelessly crippled, had to be scuttled and *Cushing* and *Monssen* burned all day before finally sinking. To cap an infamous Friday the 13th, a Japanese submarine torpedo nailed *Juneau* in the middle of the group of survivors headed for Espiritu and she disappeared in a monumental explosion which left almost no survivors.

The score at the end of the third battle of Savo Island appeared to be one battleship and two destroyers definitely sunk on the Japanese side against two light AA cruisers and four destroyers lost on the American side. There was certainly damage received by other Japanese ships, but the damage to *San Francisco* was very heavy and that to *Portland* enough to take her out of operations for several months. *Sterett* and *Aaron Ward* would also be out of action for a long time. The Japanese thrust at Henderson Field had been thwarted, but Callaghan, Scott, and a thousand other officers and men had given their lives to protect it.

The total failure of the American command was a mystery to Wright. Dan Callaghan was a fine, intelligent naval officer brought up in battleships and cruisers. He had been executive officer of *Portland,* naval aide to President Roosevelt, commanding officer of *New Orleans* and, until a month before the battle, chief of staff to Admiral Ghormley, Commander of the South Pacific Area. If anyone should have been prepared for this battle, it should have been Dan, but the tactics of the battle were essentially nonexistent. The order of ships in his column made good sense, particularly if he was going to detach the two destroyer groups as separate units while he fought the five cruisers of the center, but to push that long column into the middle of an enemy force just didn't make sense.

Wright could sympathize that Callaghan had little time to get organized, having been given the ships and task of intercepting the Japanese bombardment force only a half day before the battle started, but his only contribution to the engagement was to point his column at the enemy after the initial contact and then to head it north toward a blocking position which he never actually attained. He had withheld permission for his radar-equipped ships to engage the enemy beyond visual range, thus sacrificing the advantage of surprise, and once firing broke out, he had interrupted the battle with a confusing order in a futile attempt to prevent U.S. ships from firing into each other. Callaghan had been trying to hold tight the reins of command in a melee of two dozen ships. This obviously could not be done, particularly without the aid of the PPI of a good surface radar.

This brought up the subject of where Wright should post himself during battle; on the flag bridge where he could see, but was subject to the full blast of turret two just forward; in the armored conning tower with its periscopes but no plotting facilities; in flag plot abaft the conning tower, with all the facilities needed for communicating, navigating, plotting, and recording, but with little armor protection; or in radar plot in front of the SG, where he would have the complete radar picture, but no command facilities and no way of actually seeing what was going on. Suppose the ship were hit and lost power—he would be blind.

Although Callaghan's force had shielded Henderson from the big guns of *Hiei* and *Kirishima,* in the wee hours of Saturday the 14th, two Japanese heavy cruisers and their accompanying screen treated the field to more than a half hour of heavy bombardment, which destroyed eighteen planes and damaged twice that number, but didn't succeed in putting the field out of commission. It was a good thing, because the 14th was a day for the fliers. It began when bombers and torpedo planes from both Henderson Field and *Enterprise* found the main force from which the bombarding cruisers had come. In a series of attacks they sank the heavy cruiser *Kinugasa,* damaged the heavies *Chokai* and *Maya,* plus light cruiser *Isuzu* and destroyer *Michishio.* As they chased the survivors westward they were met by defending fighters from the carrier *Hiyo* and a savage air battle ensued, during which the remaining Japanese ships escaped toward Shortland Island.

Of more strategic importance, a force of eleven transports escorted by a dozen destroyers was discovered coming down the middle of the "Slot" north of the New Georgia Islands, heading for Guadalcanal. This was the "reinforcement force" and stopping it became the top priority. Every available American plane was thrown into action and by the end of the day seven of the heavily loaded ships had been sent to the bottom. The remaining four, all damaged, continued southeast and ran themselves aground during the night near Tassafaronga Point, sacrificing the ships to land the vital troops and supplies on Guadalcanal. The aircraft which had survived the nocturnal pounding of Henderson Field combined with those from the "Big E" in preventing the reinforcement. Even a flight of B-17s from Espiritu had helped in destroying the soldiers and equipment so desperately needed by the Japanese.

But the Japanese weren't yet ready to call it quits and another bombardment force was assembled and sent down from the north. The battleship *Kirishima,* accompanied by the heavy cruisers *Atago* and *Takao,* were to conduct the bombardment and they were screened by two light cruisers and a squadron of destroyers. This force was sighted and reported by the submarine *Trout* patrolling north of the Solomons. Admiral Lee's battleships *Washington* and *South Dakota,* accompanied by destroyers *Walke, Benham, Preston,* and *Gwin,* raced up from their standby position to intercept them.

Lee, four years senior to Wright and a bit senior to Kinkaid, was considered a gunnery expert and was as thoroughly familiar with the new radars as any senior officer in the Navy. He knew the capability of the powerful equipment of these new battleships because he had spent his professional life learning to use it. *Washington* and *South Dakota,* at 41,000 tons each, could steam at 30 knots, as compared to the 21 knots of their predecessors, and each mounted nine 16-inch rifles in three triple turrets, twenty 5-inch in ten twin mounts, more than a dozen 40-mm mounts, mostly "quads," and innumerable 20-mm barrels. He knew his two battleships were the finest fighting machines afloat.

Lee kept his two battleships together in a loose column and posted his four destroyers 5,000 yards ahead with instructions to engage without further orders once contact had been made. By 2100 on the evening of the 14th of November, Lee's column was ten miles west of Savo sweeping north looking for the bombardment force. At 2110 he changed course to the east and at 2148 headed his column southeast to pass east of Savo. Finding no Japanese lurking in Iron Bottom Bay, he swung his column due west at 2252. Eight minutes later, as *Washington* came to her new course at 15 knots, she detected a pip on her SG screen at 18,000 yards to the north, just east of Savo. Shifting to her new Mk-8 main battery radar, which provided a wonderful combined range and bearing picture of a 1,000-yard square surrounding the target, she found a pair of targets and tracked them carefully. At 2317 *Washington* opened fire almost exactly on her starboard beam, range 13,000 yards. Her salvoes straddled but didn't hit. The two Japanese ships poured on speed and headed north, making smoke as they went.

Five minutes after *Washington* opened fire, *Walke,* leading the four destroyers on a course of 300° T 5,000 yards ahead of the battleships, detected two Japanese destroyers coming around to the left of Savo Island and opened fire at 14,000 yards. *Preston* and *Benham* joined *Walke* in engaging these targets, but *Gwin* employed her battery to supply star shells over the targets being fired at by *Washington.* The Japanese replied with vigor and soon scored telling hits on *Preston,* which set her superstructure aflame. A second group of Japanese ships was following the first, and with the flames on *Preston* as a point of aim, they concentrated on the wounded ship. Their shells soon knocked out both firerooms and obliterated her after stack, bringing her to a stop. Next a salvo smashed into her quarter, spreading fire topside and causing flooding below. She quickly took a heavy list to starboard so her captain, Commander Max C. Stormes, sensing the ship was about to capsize, ordered, "Abandon ship." The crew had hardly started to go over the side before she slowly rolled over and went down by the stern. Half her crew, including Stormes, went down with her.

Walke, leading the destroyers, was closest to the approaching Japanese ships and took a number of early hits. A few minutes after *Preston* was set afire, *Walke* took a heavy salvo amidships and was almost simultaneously hit by a torpedo just forward of the bridge. The explosion blew her number two 5-inch mount high in the air and cut the ship in two. Engulfed in flames, she was dead in the water and sinking. Her skipper, Commander Thomas E. Fraser, tried to get his men off safely, but only two life rafts could be launched, so most of the survivors found themselves swimming in black oil. She went under in ten minutes, her depth charges went off, and Fraser and seventy-five of his men perished with her.

A minute after Stormes gave his last order, *Gwin,* Lieutenant Commander John B. Fellows Jr., commanding, took a shell in her engine room and another further aft. As she fought to keep her engines going and maneuvered to clear the sinking *Preston,* she saw *Benham,* Lieutenant Commander John B. Taylor commanding, hit by a torpedo which ripped open her bow. *Gwin* staggered ahead to continue the action, but she began to flood forward and had to slow to 5 knots. *Walke* sank and her depth charges went off as *Benham* passed through the wreckage, killing many of the men in the water and further damaging *Benham.* Unable to continue the battle, *Benham* turned southward to disengage. *Gwin* continued ahead slowly, still fighting with her forward guns, until *South Dakota* came roaring up from astern and the surviving Japanese hauled out of range.

After driving off the ships east of Savo with a half dozen main battery salvoes, Captain Glenn B. Davis of *Washington* watched the destroyer battle evolve ahead, but had to pick targets carefully for fear of hitting friends. An additional group of Japanese had been detected by *Washington*'s SG to the west of Savo and radar plot showed it was heading southwest. Lee ordered *Washington* left to a course to pass clear of his own destroyers and to head the enemy off. Radar showed three large pips at the rear of a five-ship enemy column; the last and largest pip might be the battleship intelligence had reported. Unfortunately, *South Dakota* had been steaming astern in the blind sector of *Washington*'s SG radar and Davis had to be sure where *South Dakota* was before he engaged any target.

South Dakota, with Captain Thomas L. Gatch in command, riding slightly on *Washington*'s starboard quarter, had an internal electrical power failure just as the destroyer battle was heating up, wiping out her tactical radios and all of her search radar capability. She was blind for less than five minutes, but she missed Lee's course change and temporarily lost the picture. Engaging a Japanese light cruiser on his starboard beam, Gatch turned right to pass the destroyers and when clear came back to the initial course of 300° T. As the big ship's after turret fired deeper and deeper on the quarter, the muzzle flash set a plane afire on her starboard catapult. A later salvo blasted the blazing plane over the side, but for several minutes the flames provided a point of aim for most of the Japanese fleet. She had also been identified while silhouetted against the burning *Walke* and *Preston.*

As soon as the two battleships were clear of the shattered destroyers, they could concentrate on the main enemy column west of Savo, which had turned to a westerly course parallel to them. In a few minutes the Japanese column reversed course again to engage and *Washington,* now sure of her target, opened fire with full salvoes from her main battery at the Japanese battleship. Meanwhile, *South Dakota* was caught in the beam of a Japanese searchlight and took several large-caliber hits, one of which jammed turret three in train. Both battleships poured out intense fire from the 16-inch turrets and their numerous 5-inch dual-purpose guns. Several enemy ships were in flames and the last ship in column, now definitely identified as the Japanese battleship *Kirishima,* was hit heavily.

Two successive groups of Japanese destroyers launched torpedo attacks at *South Dakota,* but Gatch turned her away in the nick of time and none hit. The topside damage from Japanese shells, however, was becoming increasingly serious. Many of her gun control stations were out of commission, she had only one gunnery radar still operating, and she was still out of radio communication with the flagship. When it was clear that the Japanese column had turned away, Captain Gatch, a classmate and close friend of Wright's, had turned southward to retire.

Lee, in the still undamaged *Washington,* continued westward at 25 knots, hammering at the remainder of the Japanese column, now 15,000 yards abaft his starboard beam on a parallel course. The burning *Kirishima* had dropped out of the action and was disappearing astern. At 20 minutes past midnight, just over an hour since *Washington* first opened fire, Lee ordered Davis to come right to a more northerly course to press the enemy. After ten more minutes of long-range dueling, when the range had dropped to 10,000 yards, the Japanese heavies had had enough and turned away, making smoke. Almost simultaneously, two Japanese destroyers appeared from the north, so Lee turned his flagship about and zigzagged away from the new menace. He chose a course to the southeast to skirt the Russell Islands and keep any pursuing Japanese away from his cripples. *Gwin,* having put out the fires and gotten her flooding under control, was shepherding *Benham* southward, but it was no use. *Benham* had to be abandoned by late afternoon and *Gwin,* after removing Taylor and his crew, shot four torpedoes at her with no success, and finally sank her with gunfire. *Washington* and *South Dakota* joined at a pre-arranged rendezvous at 0900 and proceeded together to Nouméa.

Ching Lee had certainly handled his battle more skillfully than his predecessors, but the results of the action weren't clear. On our side we had lost three destroyers with heavy damage to the fourth. *South Dakota* had taken more than 40 major caliber hits and lost a number of men. The Japanese had lost *Kirishima* and one destroyer for certain, and there must have been heavy damage on the two heavy cruisers in the column with the battleship and probably to many of the escorting destroyers and light cruisers.

But now it was Wright's turn. He would certainly be alert and ready as he entered Iron Bottom Bay. He had gotten rid of his airplanes. He had conferred with Rear Admiral Mahlon S. Tisdale, second in command of TF-67, and all of his skippers yesterday, when the force was first put on twelve hours' notice, to get their latest thoughts and clear up any questions they had. All commanders were unanimous in their advice to keep the TBS clear of everything except urgent messages and tactical orders. He had gone over his plan of positioning the four destroyers ahead and releasing them early to attack with torpedoes. He had explained his intention of keeping his cruisers about 10,000 yards from the enemy and maneuvering them by turn signals. And he had given every skipper permission to open fire when within 6,000 yards of an enemy. He had certainly made it clear that when he gave an order to commence firing, he meant it.

Having reviewed everything available on the past engagements, having probed for every mistake made in previous actions, it was now time to make sure his battle plan was as complete as possible and that his instructions were clear. He swung his feet down from his footrest, descended from his admiral's throne and stepped through the door to flag plot where his staff was busy with last-minute preparations. He needed to review the traffic to see if any new information had come in.

∼ II ∼

THE PLAN

Rear Admiral Thomas C. Kinkaid had relieved Rear Admiral Raymond A. Spruance as Commander Cruiser Division (ComCruDiv) Five after the Battle of Midway and had commanded Task Force Sixteen, with *Enterprise* at its center, through the invasion of the Solomon Islands and the struggles which ensued. *Enterprise,* severely damaged during the battles of Stewart Island and Santa Cruz, was the only remaining U.S. carrier in the combat area. She had been operating continuously since the beginning of the war and was overdue for a complete overhaul. Admiral Halsey was understandably reluctant to commit his one remaining carrier task force, so when the disasters of mid-November eliminated Callaghan and Scott, Halsey sent Kinkaid forward to replace them. He had arrived at Espíritu Santo in his flagship *Northampton* to take command of the newly formed Task Force Sixty-Seven on 24th of November and immediately set to work to organize his force for the coming battles. Four heavy cruisers, two light cruisers, and eight destroyers were assigned to his command and he had two top-notch deputies in two rear admirals, Wright and Tisdale.

By the 27th he had completed and distributed his Operation Plan No. 1-42 to guide his subordinates in the expected operations. He planned to divide his six cruisers into three two-ship task units, each under an admiral and each containing at least one SG surface search radar. He planned to make a similar division of his destroyers when they were assembled.

Wright had worked with Kinkaid in the development of his Plan and concurred with every part of it. When, the day after his OpPlan was issued, Kinkaid got emergency orders from the commander in chief, Admiral King, it took little time to turn command of Task Force Sixty-Seven over to Wright. Next day intelligence indicated a Japanese re-supply effort was imminent and TF-67 was put on twelve hours' notice by Commander South Pacific (ComSoPac). Wright, with no time for elaborate paperwork, had simply marked up Kinkaid's OpPlan in red pencil to reflect the number of ships he actually had and issued it to his commanders at the planning conference. With five cruisers and two admirals, he reassigned one of the cruisers which would have been in Kinkaid's task unit to each of the other task units. Should it be desirable to divide his cruisers, he would take *Minneapolis, New Orleans,* and *Pensacola* in his task unit and Tisdale would have *Honolulu* and *Northampton* under his command. With only four destroyers and no commodore, he put all of them under command of the senior skipper, Commander W. M. Cole in *Fletcher,* but he had confidence in Cole—he had certainly handled his ship well that terrible night when Callaghan and Scott were lost.

At 1940 on the 29th an urgent message from ComSoPac instructed Wright to prepare to depart, with whatever ships available, to intercept an enemy force of eight destroyers and six transports expected to arrive at Guadalcanal on the night of the 30th. At 2240 he received orders to proceed and pass through Lengo Channel off the north coast of Guadalcanal to arrive at Tassafaronga, a point of land halfway between Lunga Point and Cape Esperance, at 2300 the next night. There was no time to lose. His destroyers were underway in 30 minutes and his cruisers followed as soon as the destroyers were clear. Segond Channel at Espiritu Santo was a narrow, unmarked channel, and threading the tight passages through the dense minefield protecting the entrance was not easy, even in daylight. Helpfully, the senior officer present afloat (SOPA) sent lighted boats ahead to mark the critical turning points and all of his ships sortied successfully. By 0300 Task Force Sixty-Seven was clear of the New Hebrides, making 27 knots on course 315° T, headed for the Solomons.

Following Kinkaid's plan, two of the SOC single-float biplanes from each cruiser had been flown off at dawn to return to the safety of Segond Channel. The remaining two of each cruiser were to be catapulted in late afternoon to proceed ahead to Tulagi. Wright had augmented Kinkaid's general instructions to the pilots with specific orders. At 2200 that night, the ten cruiser planes at Tulagi were to take off and operate in two flights of five aircraft each. Flight One was to operate in the vicinity of Savo Island to search for enemy ships and report any contacts. Flight Two was to search the Guadalcanal coast from Cape Esperance to Tassafaronga and return to Cape Esperance to await further orders. Each plane was provided with four high-intensity parachute flares to be dropped only on specific orders from ComTaskForce 67. In case flares were ordered to illuminate the shoreline of Guadalcanal, they should be dropped at least one mile inland. Cruiser planes could be very valuable for detecting and observing the enemy; they could spot the fall of shot much more effectively than any observer on board ship, but they were fire hazards if caught on board, and misplaced flares could assist the enemy while blinding our own forces.

The most important part of Kinkaid's OpPlan was the Annex on night battle instructions, so Wright's first act after entering flag plot was to review with his staff those critical words. They read as follows:

NIGHT ACTION

1. Cruisers will form on line of bearing normal to the general bearing line, distance 1,000 yards. Destroyers will form at 4,000 yards 30° on the engaged bow of the cruiser line.

2. Initial contact should be made by radar. One or more destroyer pickets will be stationed 10,000 yards in the direction of expected contact, in order to obtain early information of the enemy. When so stationed destroyers will be ordered to take station as pickets on specified true bearings from the guide. Approach maneuvering will be ordered by TBS based on radar tracking. All maneuvers after commencement of firing by our cruisers will be ordered by TBS and secondary warning net.

3. As soon as possible destroyers will be ordered to form and attack. It is expected that destroyer torpedo attacks will be made early in order to obtain the maximum benefits of surprise. All radar facilities may be used by destroyers, and the attack should be made on radar infor-mation insofar as possible. Results of radar tracking will be furnished the destroyer commander by TBS. Destroyers must clear expeditiously and in such a positive manner that there is the least possible chance for mistaken identity. All ships having IFF must insure that it is turned on well before night action, particularly when destroyers are separated from the cruisers. On completion of torpedo attacks and after com-mencement of cruiser action, destroyers engage enemy destroyers or cruisers being engaged by our cruisers, and be prepared to provide star shell illumination if so ordered.

4. Insofar as practicable, the range will be maintained in excess of 12,000 yards until our destroyer attack has been completed. Commencement of fire will be ordered at a range of between 10,000 and 12,000 yards. Fire will be opened using fire control radars, and the distribution of fire will be normal insofar as can be determined with the radar equipment available. Intention is that cruiser planes will silhouette enemy force by flares. Visual point of aim should be used as soon as available. If fire can not be maintained with fire control radar, and visual point is not available, individual ships may illuminate with star shells. Searchlights will not be used. Ships should be prepared to spot by radar.

5. In normal action the range will be controlled by ship turns. When action is broken off the course may be reversed and the range closed in order to sink enemy cripples. In reverse action the range will be controlled by ship turns and head of column movements not in excess of 30°. The minimum range will depend upon the tactical situation and advantages gained in the early phases of the action, but in general will not be less than 6,000 yards.

6. Night fighting lights may only be used if under attack by a friendly vessel, and then only for the shortest possible time to ensure recognition.

At 0630 Wright had originated a message to all of his subordinates stating his best estimate of the situation as:

INFORMATION ENEMY FORCES ESTIMATED 8 DESTROYERS, 6 TRANSPORTS PROBABLY ATTEMPTING LAND REINFORCEMENTS TASSAFARONGA AREA 2300 TONIGHT X WILL PROCEED THROUGH LENGO CHANNEL AND DESTROY ENEMY.

He had followed at 0840 with:

PRESENT INTENTION DESTROYERS CONCENTRATE TWO MILES AHEAD OF GUIDE BEFORE ENTERING LENGO CHANNEL. UPON CLEARING CHANNEL AND UNTIL CONTACT IS MADE DESTROYERS ON BEARING 300 TRUE FROM GUIDE DISTANCE TWO MILES. CRUISERS IN LINE OF BEARING 320. MANEUVER BY TURN SIGNALS TO PASS ABOUT 6 MILES FROM COAST. EXPECT TO DIRECT

COMMENCE GUN FIRE AT RANGE ABOUT 12000 YARDS. SITU-
ATION WILL PROBABLY NOT PERMIT WITHHOLDING GUN-
FIRE TO COMPLETE TORPEDO ATTACKS. ANY VESSEL HAVING
KNOWN ENEMY WITHIN SIX THOUSAND YARDS IS AUTHORIZED
TO OPEN FIRE.

Information from air reconnaissance, coastwatchers, and radio intercepts trickled in all day and were immediately relayed from ComSoPac in Nouméa, but the exact composition of the approaching enemy force never crystallized. The enemy desperately needed men and supplies to sustain his struggle ashore at "Cactus." He had made heroic attempts to get reinforcements to his beleaguered troops and had taken heavy losses in the process. There had been sightings of destroyer groups and an occasional cruiser during the day, but none heading directly for Guadalcanal.

Where were the transports and cargo vessels? What was needed ashore couldn't be carried in destroyers—tanks, heavy artillery, adequate ammunition is heavy stuff. If the Japanese were going to hold out on Guadalcanal they would need heavy transport. Where was it? The enemy must have some harbor up the line where he could hide the vital supply ships and move them down the island chain at night. The prime targets to be intercepted were the transports. The battle for Guadalcanal had become a contest of supplies. Every ton of material delivered to our troops ashore had been contested. The latest event was the torpedoing of the attack cargo ship *Alchiba* by a Japanese midget submarine on the day before Task Force Sixty-Seven had sailed. According to the last messages from Guadalcanal, she might still be burning.

As the day wore on, the sky darkened and became overcast. There were intermittent rain squalls and visibility was occasionally limited. About 1600 the rain began to let up, so Wright decided to get the SOCs on their way. They needed time to find their way through the weather and get settled in Tulagi before dark.

Wright spent the next two hours studying the charts of the area, especially the upper Solomons. He tried to imagine what the Japanese commander might be doing. It was obvious that command of the overall area was handled at Rabaul, on New Britain Island in the Bismarck Archipelago, 560 miles to the northwest, but there had been a great deal of activity in the Buin-Shortland area recently. The Japanese had an airstrip there from which their fighters had to operate for any activity over Guadalcanal, but there never seemed to be any ships there. Destroyers, cruisers, tankers, and supply ships had been sighted daily, heading toward or away from the area, but when reconnaissance planes passed over or we sent in attacks with long-range bombers, they seldom seemed to catch any Japanese ships. During the big efforts against Guadalcanal, heavy forces were contacted moving down from Truk, a thousand miles to the north, but it was a mystery where the smaller forces hid during daylight hours.

By 1800 the rain had stopped and the sky was partly overcast with a light wind from the east. Wright moved out of flag plot to the port wing of the signal bridge. It was just about sunset and they were now abreast of San Cristobal and the 27-knot breeze from the ship's speed was refreshing—he needed a cool head for the coming hours. The ship's navigator had reported they were actually making more than 28 knots over the ground, so he had arrived at Koli Point on time. If he had only gotten his orders to intercept six hours earlier, say before sunset on the 29th, he would have had time to pass Guadalcanal to the south and cut off any enemy force before it reached Savo instead of having to meet the enemy in Iron Bottom Bay, in the narrow waters between Guadalcanal and Tulagi. At least ComNavTulagi had radioed that the PT boats would be held in port for the night. That eliminated one uncertainty as he searched for the enemy.

But it served no purpose to worry about what might have been. He would have to thread the needle through Lengo Channel and take what was coming. Had he thought of everything? He had ordered the fighting lights to be green-over-white-over-white. He had ordered screened wake lights to be used. What else was there to think of? He was not only alone as he stood on the bridge wing studying Malaita Island ahead on his starboard bow; he felt alone.

As the dark of night descended, Guadalcanal loomed large on the port bow and Wright shifted his screening destroyers into a column ahead of the cruisers. At 2000 he ordered all ships to battle stations. Silence replaced light as the vigil of the night commenced.

The *Minneapolis'* Sail George radar would now be the eyes to let him see through the dark. On the front of the SG control console in radar plot, two decks below the flag bridge, was a 10-inch diameter plan position indicator (PPI) scope on which a ray of green luminescence rotated about its center following the motions of the SG antenna on the foremast. It painted a picture of the surroundings as though the observer were high above the ship looking down. It could be set for true bearing so that the top of the scope was north as on a normal map or nautical chart, or it could be set on relative bearing, giving a picture with the ship's bow at the top. The beam of the SG was sufficiently narrow to paint a single ship as a blip only 3° wide and it was designed to scan the surface of the water like a beam of light. When set on long range it could show targets out to 75,000 yards and, on short range, out to 15,000 yards. Though it had a bearing scale around the scope and the operator could turn on range markers to trace range circles every successive mile out from the center, to measure range and bearing accurately, the operator had to stop the rotation of the antenna, scan the beam across the target a couple of times to find the center, then run his range pipper to the center of the target blip, and read the measured range and bearing before resuming the scan. This took a few seconds for each range and bearing and the picture on the PPI was lost during such pauses. In general the admiral and the captain wanted the SG scanning all of the time to show them the tactical situation while the gunnery and torpedo officers wanted precision.

A U.S. supply force of three transports and five destroyers was coming east through Lengo Channel with orders to be clear of Iron Bottom Bay during the expected action, and two of the destroyers, *Lamson,* Lieutenant Commander Philip H. Fitz-Gerald commanding (with ComDesDiv 9 embarked) and *Lardner,* Lieutenant Commander William M. Sweetzer commanding, were ordered by ComSoPac to join Task Force Sixty-Seven at the entrance to Lengo. Wright's column met the outgoing group in the dark just where the channel got narrow. With all ships' steaming darkened and the difficulty of radar detection so close to the island, there were moments of doubt as to identity. There were also some near collisions as the two forces passed each other. Wright slowed to 20 knots, then to 15 for safety.

ComDesDiv 9, Commander Laurence A. Abercrombie with his two ships, reported for duty as instructed and Wright ordered them to fall in astern of the cruisers. There was no practical way to pass copies of his OpPlan to the newcomers and contact with the enemy could occur at any moment. Though the TBS was considered secure, it would be foolhardy to pass his entire battle instructions over any radio circuit. Passing the instructions by blinker gun would take the better part of an hour. He would just have to depend on good sense and tactical signals when the time came.

Lengo Channel narrowed to just under two miles wide between Guadalcanal and the outlying reefs and as Wright's long column sliced through at 20 knots, the pungent smell of the jungle flowers reached out to the men topside, they were that close to the beach. When *Minneapolis* came abreast of Koli Point where he was sure he was past the reefs, Wright ordered his cruiser column right to 320° T to parallel the distant coast of Guadalcanal to the left as well as the shoal line off Florida Island on his right. Cole's destroyers, 4,000 yards ahead, came to a parallel course. When his ships were in deep water and sufficiently clear of the coast, he ordered all ships to turn simultaneously to 280° T to head directly toward Cape Esperance, 25 miles to westward. Eleven ships in quarter echelon sweeping across the sound, searching for the enemy, even in the dark, was impressive. Wright could see the faint luminescence of the bow waves of the succession of ships stretching out on the port quarter. He stared through the dark with his binoculars, searching for a telltale trace of the enemy. If intelligence was correct, the Japanese transports should be nearing the beach off the port bow. Any destroyers should be screening to seaward. It was a very dark night. By checking his ability to see his other ships, Wright judged the visibility to be about two miles—4,000 yards.

Rear Admiral Carleton H. Wright, U.S. Navy, first on right, with Admiral W. F. Halsey Jr., Admiral Royal E. Ingersoll, and other dignitaries at ceremonies to honor the Third Fleet, San Francisco, 16 October 1945. Photo from Naval Historical Center, Washington Navy Yard.

USS Minneapolis *(CA-36), firing battle practice on 29 March 1939, as seen from her embarked aviation unit VCS-6. Photo from National Archives.*

USS New Orleans *(CA-32), photo taken 18 days before the battle. Photo from U.S. Naval Institute, James C. Fahey Collection.*

USS Pensacola *(CA-24), 28 September 1942. Photo from U.S. Naval Institute, James C. Fahey Collection.*

USS Honolulu *(CL-48), pre-war photo without radar. Photo from U.S. Naval Institute.*

USS Fletcher *(DD-445), at anchor in Purvis Bay, Florida Island, Solomons, 26 March 1943. Photo from Naval Historical Center.*

USS Perkins *(DD-377). Pre-war photo from U.S. Naval Institute.*

USS Maury *(DD-401), fueling from USS* South Dakota, *27 October 1942, following the Battle of the Santa Cruz Islands. Photo from National Archives.*

USS Maury *(DD-401), departing Segond Channel, Espiritu Santo, 6 February 1943. Official Navy Photo.*

USS Drayton *(DD-366), Mare Island Navy Yard, 14 April 1942. Photo from U.S. Naval Institute, James C. Fahey Collection.*

USS Lamson *(DD-367). Photo from U.S. Naval Institute, James C. Fahey Collection.*

USS Lardner *(DD-487), Federal Shipbuilding and Dry Dock Co., Kearny, N.J., 12 May 1942. Photo from U.S. Naval Institute, James C. Fahey Collection.*

⟋ III ⟍
THE BATTLE

At 2306, *Minneapolis*'s radar plot reported two radar pips off Cape Esperance bearing 284°, distance 23,000 yards. Wright had this contact broadcast to all ships over the TBS and ordered a simultaneous turn of all ships back to course 320°, putting the cruisers and the lead destroyers into two columns, 4,000 yards apart. *Fletcher, Perkins,* then *New Orleans* confirmed the contacts and began to amplify. The number of ships reported to be in the target group jumped to four, then six.

Wright ordered his cruiser column to course 300°, but kept his speed at 20 knots. He studied the positions of the enemy being plotted by his staff navigator on the chart on the big table in the center of flag plot. They were falling in a line parallel to the coast of Guadalcanal, about two miles out from the beach. The relative plot being kept by the flag lieutenant began to indicate a beam range of 7,000 yards. It looked good. The range was already closing rapidly and 20 knots was a good speed for gunnery. Radar reported the enemy in a column of four ships close to the shore of Guadalcanal—course 140°, speed 16, with two ships about 2,000 yards to seaward. Were they the transports or an advance group of destroyers? Or both?

At 2316, by TBS, Cole requested permission to fire torpedoes. Wright checked with radar plot—range to the closest target was still 14,600 yards. An Mk-15 torpedo could only go 4,800 yards at high speed. Wright replied, "Range to our bogey is excessive." *Northampton* clogged the TBS momentarily with a report of a flashing signal from Tassafaronga. Wright queried Cole, "Do you have them located?" Cole came back, "Affirmative. Range is all right for us." It didn't check. Perhaps Cole was on a different target. Wright called radar plot again to see if there was any change in the picture, any indication of which were the transports. Could plot distinguish between the targets—were some ships larger than others? The seconds multiplied into minutes while he waited. The radar officer saw some movement but wasn't sure. He was sure of four targets and guessed they were destroyers.

Wright's instincts told him no commander would send his precious transports ahead of their escort. These must be an advance group of destroyers. The range was still over 12,000 yards but closing fast. He shared his conclusion with Cole, "Suspect bogies are DDs. We now have four." Realizing he couldn't wait any longer he finally sent, "Go ahead and fire torpedoes." Cole relayed it to the lead destroyers. Wright checked again with radar plot. The range to the closest target was now 10,000 yards and dropping. He picked up the TBS handset and gave the crucial order to all ships, "Stand by to roger." Then, after a slight pause, "Execute roger. And I do mean roger!"

At 2310 *Fletcher*'s SG had picked up the targets at 14,000 yards and Cole, ordering the lead destroyers to increase speed to 25 knots, had stepped back into the radar room just abaft the pilot house to see the PPI for himself. His executive officer, Lieutenant Commander Joseph C. Wylie Jr., was running the show and already had a plot going on the small DRT plotting table, a novelty found only in this newest class of destroyer. Within two minutes the enemy formation became clear: a column of several ships with a single ship riding on the port beam of the column leader. They were running parallel to the coast, about a mile and a half out. The plot showed a course of 150° T, speed 15. To make sure he wouldn't pass too far out, Cole told his OOD to bring the ship left to 290° and moved out to the port wing of the bridge to see if he could see anything with his binoculars.

Cole had spent a lot of time thinking about night actions, particularly after his experience two weeks before on the night *San Francisco* got shot up. He had organized *Fletcher* to make the most of her great SG radar and he believed in deliberate, planned action. He had told the other destroyer skippers at the conference of his intention to use the intermediate speed setting of 36 knots, planning a torpedo run of about 6,000 yards. This would keep our ships far enough away from the enemy to avoid visual detection, but the torpedo run would still be well within intermediate speed range.

Instructing radar plot to select *Fletcher*'s target in accordance with normal distribution rules, he moved to the port torpedo director and watched the torpedo officer set up the Mk-27 director for the first half-salvo of five fish. The spread of 1° between torpedoes would place a warhead every hundred yards along the target's track—about the length of a destroyer. He then moved forward to the port pelorus to probe the dark with his binoculars, where he could see the pelorus' compass rose for true bearings. The torpedo officer called out the computed target track angle as it changed following the bearings from the radar. As it approached 270° for the perfect beam shot, Cole picked up the TBS handset and transmitted "Interrogatory William," requesting permission to fire torpedoes. Range to the target at that moment was about 7,000 yards. Wright's negative reply puzzled him, but perhaps the admiral could see something he couldn't. He watched the bearing drift aft and waited. A golden opportunity was slipping by! Cole checked with radar—the SG now showed a column of four targets with the flanker moving back to almost the middle of the column. The track showed a course of 140°, speed 15. Cole waited with growing concern.

At 2320 Wright finally gave permission, a full five minutes after his request. He immediately relayed the order to his other ships, but held his own fire to check the solution on the Mk-27. The center of the enemy column was now 7,300 yards on his port beam, but his torpedoes would have to run over 8,000 yards to catch the enemy—too far for intermediate. Cole ordered torpedo speed to low—27 knots, gave the torpedo men time to make the change, then ordered, "Fire torpedoes." The first fish sprang into the water off the port quarter, and the others followed at 3-second intervals—Cole hoped they would reach.

Fletcher's first half-salvo had hardly hit the water when Wright's order to commence fire came in. Cole held up his guns until he fired the second half-salvo, this time at the second ship from the head of the column. With all ten of his torpedoes safely on their way, he ordered his gunnery officer to open fire on the right-hand target of the enemy formation.

Perkins, following 500 yards astern in *Fletcher*'s wake, had made contact at almost the same moment as *Fletcher,* plotted the enemy on course 125° T, speed 15, and fired a full salvo of eight fish at the closest enemy, the flanker, then 5,000 yards abeam.

Maury, with no SG radar, could find no target, so Captain Sims (Lieutenant Commander Gelzer L. Sims) held his torpedoes for a better moment.

Drayton's SG had detected a group of five targets even before *Fletcher* announced her contact, but she shifted to some additional targets at 16,000 yards, to the right of the initial group. After several minutes of plotting indicated a target speed of zero, Captain Cooper (Lieutenant Commander James E. Cooper) doubted the validity of his contact, so when the order was received to fire torpedoes, he fired only two at a range of 8,000 yards and saved the rest for later use.

Within seconds after the first torpedo hit the water the three massive turrets of *Minneapolis* roared out in unison. The blast almost knocked Captain Charles E. Rosendahl off his feet as he stood by the port pelorus and it did knock the headset off his talker. The flash was dazzling, lighting up the ocean for hundreds of yards. Anyone caught with his eyes open could see nothing except the brilliant orange blob the flash had etched into the retina. The concussion took the breath away. Debris from the muzzles joined dirt, dust, and paint chips from every part of the ship and showered topside. Before the second salvo crashed out, the port 5-inch battery added to the din with two salvoes of star shells, then continued to add to them every five seconds.

New Orleans opened fire within a minute and *Northampton* opened almost simultaneously. *Pensacola,* with no SG radar, took a few minutes to find a target and didn't commence firing until four minutes after *Minneapolis. Honolulu,* with her fifteen quick-firing 6-inch guns, didn't find a suitable target until a minute later.

Next to last in the long column, *Lamson,* with no orders and no target, saw where the cruisers were shooting and started firing star shells in the direction of the splashes.

Ahead, *Fletcher* got off 60 rounds of 5-inch at the last ship in the enemy column, but her FD radar lost contact, so she checked fire. Star shells streaked in from the left and filled the sky with dazzling flares from the quarter forward to the beam. As their number increased, the eerie white light brought a type of daylight to the scene. A wall of smoke and shell splashes blanketed the target area, but no ships could be seen. A few flashes, which might be gunfire, appeared to the right of the main enemy group.

Perkins fired 50 rounds of 5-inch at her torpedo target, and Captain Reed (Lieutenant Commander Walter C. Reed) observed a large explosion, perhaps from her torpedoes. The target disappeared in the smoke and spume so quickly he could observe no details. He saw flashes of gunfire well to the left of the main group of radar targets and observed they were being fired at by the cruisers astern.

Maury found a target with her FD radar about the time "commence fire" was received and developed a solution of course 120°, speed 12. As she opened fire, her FD shorted out with a great flash, so she continued, using only the range-keeper's solution, for 20 salvoes, rocking them back and forth across the target, hoping for hits. She momentarily saw her target through the smoke, despite the blinding glare of the star shells between her and the enemy, but it was quickly obscured. Her best guess at identity was "small merchantman."

Drayton stuck to her target to the right of the others, now at 6,700 yards and still tracking at zero speed. She opened fire with two salvoes of star shells set to burst at 12,000 yards, well behind her target, and followed with almost a hundred rounds of 5-inch fired to hit. She never saw the enemy nor any result of her firing.

With all of his torpedoes expended and no targets in sight, Cole continued westward at 25 knots hoping for explosions when his slow torpedoes finally reached the enemy. About 5 minutes after firing his fish, an enemy salvo of three shells hit the water just 100 yards ahead of *Fletcher* and was followed by another 200 yards to port. Cole brought *Fletcher* sharply right to course 350° T and increased speed to 30 knots.

Captain Reed in *Perkins* sighted a torpedo crossing his bow, then his ship was straddled by incoming shells—of fairly large caliber, judging from the size of the splashes. He increased speed and made smoke as he followed *Fletcher* northward. *Maury* and *Drayton* both sighted torpedo wakes and shell splashes, but none of the lead destroyers was hit.

As the four destroyers raced northward, heading just to the left of Savo itself, large explosions were reported all along the Guadalcanal beach—their torpedoes were finally hitting something.

Minneapolis's second 8-inch salvo appeared to be a direct hit and the third and fourth were straddles. By this time the star shell illumination was becoming effective and, although some observers thought the target was a destroyer or cruiser, the captain and the gunnery officer saw only one stack and a merchantman's bow; they identified it as a transport. It was observed to explode and could no longer be seen, so they checked fire and shifted right to another target. This one, at 10,500 yards, was identified as a destroyer with a single stack, very much like U.S. destroyers. Four salvoes were poured into it and a full salvo from a cruiser astern was seen to merge with the last one from *Minneapolis,* plowing into the middle of the enemy ship at the same time, breaking it in two. Its bow and stern were seen to rise out of the water and the ship disappeared. Fire was checked and the main battery shifted left to a third target, identified as a large destroyer or cruiser, already being engaged by others. She added a single salvo and it also disappeared.

New Orleans opened on the same target at which *Minneapolis* was first firing, identifying it as a destroyer leading the enemy column. She saw it blow up and disappear after four salvoes. Her next target was identified as an *Atago*-class cruiser and it was seen to explode after three or four salvoes had landed. Fire was then shifted left to a cargo ship which could be seen by the light of the now numerous star shells. After the second salvo, this ship blew up with a tremendous explosion and continued to burn fiercely. Swinging left again, her guns found another cargo ship close to the beach and after her second salvo this ship too exploded and burned.

Pensacola, with no SG, had trouble finding a target, but as the star shell illumination improved, she found one optically and opened fire at 10,000 yards. Though she observed her salvoes straddling, it was only after she used her own 5-inch for illumination that she was able to identify her adversary as a three-stack Japanese light cruiser. The target appeared damaged and heavily listing to port. After her fifth salvo, a large explosion occurred and the ship disappeared. A target was then found by FC radar at 8,000 yards to the right of the first target. As *Pensacola* opened fire, it came clearly into sight, apparently emerging from a smoke screen. It was immediately identified as a *Mogami*- or *Yubari*-class cruiser and, as *Pensacola*'s second salvo bore in just abaft her single stack, the ship exploded and disappeared. With no other targets in sight, *Pensacola* unloaded her main battery "through the muzzle" and awaited developments.

Honolulu took her time sorting out possible targets and finally settled on a good one about five minutes after the shooting started. She picked one to the left of the blazing ship set afire by *Minneapolis* and *New Orleans* and opened with a straddle. She cut her ranging ladder short and shifted to rapid, continuous fire, each individual gun firing as soon as loaded. A bridge of red tracers arced into the target for 30 seconds, so she checked fire to observe the effect. Her gunners couldn't actually see the target because of the glare of the star shells and the gathering smoke and haze, but, as they continued to track by radar, the rangekeeper showed the target was slowing down. She gave it another blast of rapid fire, and the target speed dropped to zero.

Northampton found a target with her FC radar to the left of the one being fired on by the two lead cruisers. As the illumination improved she identified it as a destroyer leading two light cruisers in column. She opened fire at 11,000 yards and soon observed hits. Her gunners were sure they sank it. *Lamson,* with no SG, found no targets but continued to fire star shells and followed in the wake of the cruisers. *Lardner* got in a half dozen shots at a momentary target, but lost it immediately.

Seven minutes after her first salvo, the bow of *Minneapolis* was blasted off with a huge explosion. Flames leapt skyward and sheets of water surged over her masthead, drenching everything topside. The whole hull bucked and heaved and shook like a huge wet dog. The deluge from the first explosion had hardly hit the deck when a wall of water was thrown up to port by an explosion amidships. The big ship heaved over to starboard and dug the stub of her bow deep in the water. A foot of water sloshed about the pilot house as bruised seamen struggled to regain their feet. The forecastle was ablaze and fumes from gasoline and oil swept aft to the fantail. She quickly lost way and was unable to steer. The wreckage of her bow dragged her around to the right.

Captain Clifford H. Roper in *New Orleans* astern ordered "right full rudder" to clear the flaming flagship. His ship had hardly begun to respond when a titanic explosion erupted between turret one and turret two. The entire bow, including turret one, was torn off and floated down the port side, gouging her hull and tearing a blade off number four propeller as it passed. The stricken ship convulsed with a loping motion that threw men off their feet. All power was lost forward. She slowed rapidly and settled by the bow.

The executive officer, Commander W. F. Riggs Jr., in secondary conn high in the after superstructure, saw the flames and burning debris reach twice as high as the foremast—oily water poured into the top of his station. He felt certain that a magazine had exploded and everyone forward had been wiped out. Unable to raise the bridge on any telephone circuit, he rang the steering alarm, shifted rudder control to steering aft, and took the conn. He ordered "right rudder" to bring the enemy astern and minimize the chance of a torpedo hit. With no TBS and no instructions from the captain, he scanned the exploding darkness to get his bearings.

In *Pensacola,* Captain Frank L. Lowe had habitually taken station in sky forward, a level above the bridge, to have better visibility during an air attack. He commanded the ship's armament from there while his executive officer, Commander Harry Keeler Jr., remained in the pilot house to conn the ship. When flames leaped skyward from *Minneapolis* and then *New Orleans, Pensacola*'s gunners were looking for a new target to port, so Keeler brought her head 20° to the left to clear the damaged ships. As the ship surged past her flaming sisters, he could see the devastation topside and feel the heat of the conflagration. As *Pensacola* came abreast of *Minneapolis* and Keeler ordered his helmsman to return to the original course, the ship felt the blast of a full salvo from *Minneapolis*; the 8-inch shells skimmed just over her stacks. The flagship was wounded, but not dead. As *Pensacola* ploughed into the darkness, now at the head of the cruiser column, her FC radar found a fast-moving target on the port bow at 6,000 yards and she resumed fire with her main battery. She saw flashes from her target, but never the entire ship. She was firing under full radar control and was unable to be sure of the fall of shot. The target disappeared after her seventh salvo at a range of 7,000 yards, so Captain Lowe judged the target had been destroyed and began to search for a new one. After a few sweeps of the forward director, another target was found by the FC, farther away, broad on the port bow at 12,000 yards. Careful tracking showed a target course of 295° T, speed 32 knots. *Pensacola* sent three full 8-inch salvoes to hurry it on its way, but lost radar contact and couldn't regain it. She saw some flashes in the direction of the target, but couldn't be sure that she had gotten any hits.

A ship was sighted to starboard, so *Pensacola* fired two stars over her for identification. It was *Honolulu,* which promptly flashed her fighting lights. Some splashes appeared close aboard on the port bow, seeming to be of small caliber, and as Lowe and his gunners were searching for the source, *Pensacola* shuddered from a huge explosion at the base of her mainmast. Flames and black oil shot high in the air and the ship shook with a vibration that tossed men about so violently they had to hold on to keep from being thrown to the deck. All power was lost to the turrets and the lighting throughout the ship failed. Steering was lost and the ship slowed to a crawl. Flames roared up the mainmast and engulfed the after stack. She heeled over 13°, lowering her port scuppers almost to the water's edge. The flames increased in intensity and spread both forward and aft, but the firemains were severed and there was no water.

Although the primary damage had been to the engineering spaces, she still had one fireroom and one engine room intact. Rapid action by the engineers isolated ruptured pipes, rerouted fuel oil, feed water, and steam and restored power to one shaft and some of the generators. With no targets in sight and no real ability to fight, *Pensacola* headed for Tulagi, steering by magnetic compass. Within an hour, her engineers had redistributed her fuel and had her on an even keel, but the fires topside burned for seven hours.

When *Pensacola* sheered to the left and he could clearly see the mayhem ahead, Captain Robert H. Hayler of *Honolulu* ordered, "Right full rudder" and rang up turns for 30 knots. He brought his rudder amidships as his ship's head passed through north, then turned left a little to let his 6-inch turrets continue to work on their second target, now deep on the port quarter. He presumed the ships ahead had been torpedoed and wanted to get his ship beyond the reach of any enemy torpedo. He checked fire when the damaged ships blocked the line of fire to his target, but felt confident that the hail of shells *Honolulu* had administered had sent it to a watery grave. By the time he had opened range enough to return to the base course of 300°, he could find no new targets, but kept his engines turning for 30 knots—it was a better fighting speed. He ordered a couple of star shells spreads from his 5-inch battery, but finding nothing, *Honolulu* fell silent at 2336.

Northampton turned right when *Honolulu* sheered out ahead of her, but she did not increase speed. When *Honolulu* came back a bit, she did the same, settling on course 350° T. She found a target in the direction of the opening gap between *Pensacola* and the burning cruisers and engaged it with deliberate salvoes. She came left to 320° to bring her target more on the beam and observed several salvoes hit. Director one, which had been in control of main battery train for the entire action, saw the target explode and sink, so *Northampton* checked fire after a total of 18 nine-gun salvoes. With two large destroyers definitely sunk by her guns and having seen another ship, thought to be a light cruiser, explode at a shorter range, Captain Willard A. Kitts was confident his ship had done her part.

Since she was heading directly toward Savo Island four miles away, Kitts brought his ship left to 280° to pass clear and looked for more targets. *Honolulu* had disappeared ahead, he could see the fires of *Pensacola* about 4,000 yards on his port beam, the diminishing flames of *Minneapolis* and *New Orleans* deep on his port quarter, a funeral pyre of an enemy ship to the southeast on the horizon, and at least two burning ships beyond, near the Guadalcanal shore.

At 2348, some 20 minutes after *Minneapolis* was hit, Kitts saw two torpedoes approaching sharp on his port bow and ordered, "Left full rudder." One torpedo was running at a depth of about 10 feet and the other moving very close to the surface. One or both hit aft on the port quarter and a tremendous explosion ripped open *Northampton*'s side. Her after engine room immediately flooded, three out of four of her propellers stopped, and all communication was lost with the after part of the ship. Flames and fuel oil gushed skyward around her mainmast and poured into the top of the after AA director. The whole ship shook violently for several seconds, breaking pumps, motors, and other equipment from their foundations and hurling them as projectiles about the ship. She immediately heeled over 10° to port and lost headway. Fire burst into the air to port of the mainmast, setting it and the boat deck aflame. The 5-inch ready service ammunition on the boat deck, as well as that in the adjacent hoist, started to burn. After about ten minutes the engineers got number one shaft turning again and the ship started moving slowly, swinging left. Kitts hoped to get her to safety at Tulagi, but bulkheads were failing and the list was increasing ominously.

In *Lamson,* Captain Fitz-Gerald tried to follow the tail end cruisers to the north, but had hardly come to his new course when *Northampton*'s starboard machine gunners, believing they were seeing their first enemy, opened fire on his ship. He turned sharp right, poured on the coal and cleared to the east.

Captain Sweetzer, in *Lardner,* seeing the congestion ahead, had sheered left to get clear and continued around in a 270° turn. As he steadied on 350° T to parallel the others, he too was treated to a dose of gunfire by eager cruiser gunners, so he also retired to the east.

Ahead, the lead destroyers watched in disbelief as towering flames reached skyward where the cruiser column had been. There were no orders and no reports. Cole rang up turns for 35 knots and led his ships around Savo Island. The last sight of action in the battle area was an arc of red tracers from left to right, reaching into a spot of orange flame, veiled in the smoke and haze.

Drayton's sensitive SG picked up three targets near Cape Esperance moving rapidly to the west. The range was 12,000 yards, but a plot of the speed triangle showed a torpedo run at low speed could still reach. Captain Cooper ordered a spread of four fish. At least one explosion was reported by the torpedomen when the clock said the fish should have reached the target, but Cooper doubted he had hit an enemy, since he saw no flash or flames.

Cole led his four destroyers to the north, then northeast, skirting Savo about two miles out. At 2349 a tremendous explosion directly behind Savo lighted up the southeastern sky. It was bigger and brighter than anything which had preceded it. It must have been an ammunition ship.

Having searched to the west and north of Savo, making sure no more enemy forces were in those areas, Cole headed east toward Tulagi. When he came clear of Savo and his radars could once again probe the battle area, he split his force in two sections, 3,000 yards apart, and turned south in a standard search and attack formation, *Fletcher* and *Perkins* to the east, *Maury* and *Drayton* to the west. He slowed to 15 knots to give time to evaluate contacts. There were several fires along the horizon ahead, but they weren't necessarily the danger. He was looking for undamaged enemies in the inky dark against the loom of Guadalcanal.

When the sudden explosion shattered his flagship's bow and brought her to a halt, several minutes elapsed before Wright had enough information to make any decision. With no radar, doubtful radio, and flames and water covering topside, *Minneapolis* was no place from which to command, and *New Orleans* astern was reported to have suffered a similar fate. The action was moving too rapidly to consider shifting to another ship, so when electric power failed at 2333, Wright ordered his second-in-command, Tisdale, to take over, but the flagship's TBS had died with the power; the order didn't get out.

Slicing westward in *Honolulu* at 30 knots, Tisdale endured the silence for ten minutes, then reported his course to the task force commander and requested instructions. Silence. As *Honolulu* cleared Savo Island close aboard to starboard, he ordered her right to 345° T to search to the northwest. She had hardly turned to the new course when *Northampton* exploded astern.

Minneapolis and *New Orleans* were certainly too damaged to fight. He had seen *Pensacola* hit and now *Northampton* must be gone. He tried the TBS to *Pensacola:* "Can you move?" No answer. No radio communication and no radar contact. Tisdale decided to take charge. He instructed *Honolulu* to continue around Savo Island and search to the east.

At one minute before midnight, a general signal "to any ship" was received from *Minneapolis:* "We need assistance." The gallant ship, which had continued to fire all three turrets until power was lost, had come back to life. Two minutes later, Wright's order to Tisdale to take charge was finally transmitted and received. The task force had been without an effective commander for just over thirty minutes.

Tisdale continued eastward for ten minutes, then came right to 145° T to search the center of Iron Bottom Bay. He directed the lead destroyers to join *Honolulu,* but *Fletcher* couldn't find *Honolulu* on her radar. She asked for *Honolulu*'s bearing from Savo. *Drayton,* with her SG still outperforming all others, told her the new flagship was to the northeast of Savo. A searchlight scanned from the south, so Tisdale reversed course to the northwest to get out of the beam and told Cole to join him later. Cole continued south, probing the darkness. A quarter moon had risen at 0009 and weak moonlight began to add silver to the haze.

At 0030, having swept to south of a line through Savo, Cole turned his search formation east and asked Tisdale, "Where are the other units?" Tisdale replied, "Do not know position of other units." With *Honolulu*'s last reported position to the north of him, Cole turned his formation to 000° T and increased speed to 20 knots.

When the ten cruiser SOCs tried to take off at 2200 in accordance with their orders, they couldn't get off the water. The flat calm of Tulagi Harbor was too much for their limited power and heavy load. Try as they might they couldn't break their pontoons free of the glassy sea. It was also dangerous making full power runs, nose high, across the small open stretches they could find in the harbor, so they turned on their running lights to help the other planes to see them.

About an hour later, two *Minneapolis* planes and one each from *New Orleans* and *Honolulu* made it into the air and flew southwest over the sound. They arrived over the battle area just after the firing broke out, but they contributed nothing toward the struggle below and were never instructed to drop flares. They did fly along the coast of Guadalcanal and between Cape Esperance and Savo a couple of times and their observations later contributed to the battle reports.

At 0037 a flight of SOCs that had gotten off the water later requested permission to illuminate a destroyer landing troops on Guadalcanal. Tisdale asked the plane for more details and came on the TBS with, "We are swinging left to fire on destroyer landing troops on Guadalcanal," ordering Cole to bring his destroyers to assist. Cole formed his ships into a column and headed southwest toward Cape Esperance to join the fray. For twenty minutes messages flew back and forth to the plane while *Honolulu* raced south around the west of Savo and Cole brought his ships from the east. Finally the plane dropped its flare and illuminated a wrecked merchantman, bow on to the beach, as well as every other ship in the area. Tisdale ordered the planes to "secure" and return to Tulagi.

Aboard *Minneapolis* repair parties worked feverishly in the dark to get their ship under control. She had come to a stop immediately after being hit—three out of four of her firerooms were completely flooded and she was having problems getting feed water to the fourth. Soon she was using saltwater to make steam. Most of her telephone circuits were cut and essential internal orders had to be handled by ingenuity, some by messenger. Though her TBS was knocked out, her SG radar miraculously came back on the line a few minutes after the shock. After a seemingly interminable time, the chief engineer reported ready to answer bells and the engines were ordered ahead. She crept ahead at about 3 knots, steering by magnetic compass, her gyros no longer usable.

Rosendahl first pointed *Minneapolis* toward Lunga Point, but shortly one engine room became unbearable from the lack of ventilation and had to be abandoned. Realizing the possibility of losing all power and drifting ashore behind the Japanese lines, at 0200 he altered course left to head for Tulagi. A little while later he almost ran into a piece of floating wreckage that was passed close aboard to starboard. It was identified as the protruding bow of a destroyer that had capsized and sunk by the stern, but had not yet completely gone under.

New Orleans, ten miles out from Tulagi Harbor, requested assistance, so *Maury* and *Perkins* were sent to help. *Perkins* fell in astern of *Maury,* and the two ships sped east at 25 knots. It was shortly after 0100 and it was hard to distinguish the sky from the sea in the hazy gloom. After about 20 minutes *Maury's* lookouts spotted something ahead, about 5,000 yards out and slightly to starboard. Captain Sims ordered his torpedo mounts out for "curved fire ahead," making a 16-fish spread possible. All guns were trained on the target. *Perkins,* following astern, had all her weapons at the ready.

At 4,000 yards, the shadows congealed enough to identify the target as a ship, but no more. To the right, it looked like a warship; to the left it looked like a bluff-bowed merchantman. Sims ordered his signalman to challenge with blinker gun—the proper answer would be a show of fighting lights or Very Stars—green, white, white. The buzzer of the blinker gun sounded the dots and dashes as the narrow ray flashed. *Maury's* bridge gang held its breath, the torpedo director was centered on the target, four torpedo mounts matched to its orders, impulse charges loaded and primed. The range had dropped to 2,500 yards and the ship ahead could be seen by naked eye; then, from the right-hand part of the stranger three Very Stars arced upward: white, green, green. Sims ordered, "Stand by to fire torpedoes," and screwed his eyes to his binoculars. From all over the stranger Very Stars rose—most were in the order green, white, white. Sims ordered, "Hold fire," and sheered left.

From the gloom emerged the form of *New Orleans,* down by the bow and missing everything forward of turret two! Sims eased *Maury* back to 15 knots and circled in, instructing *Perkins* to continue to patrol. *Maury* slowed and came close aboard *New Orleans.* A short conversation by bullhorn revealed the cruiser had extinguished her fires and had the flooding under control. She was making five knots and headed fair for Tulagi.

Up ahead a ship was burning, probably needing help more than *New Orleans.* The two destroyers continued to the east and soon could identify *Pensacola,* a smoldering fire licking up her mainmast, heeling heavily to port. She was making about 8 knots, so *Maury* screened ahead while *Perkins* went alongside to help with the fire fighting. When they got her to the entrance to Tulagi, *Perkins* stayed alongside while *Maury* went back to shepherd *New Orleans* to safety.

Northampton had been hit in her after engine room, which flooded immediately, but the explosion was so immense it ruptured all the surrounding fuel and water tanks, split the bulkhead to number four fireroom forward and opened cracks to the magazines aft. As the blast vented upward it ripped through the second and main deck compartments, filling them with flames and oil. Although all pumps were employed to their maximum capacity, her initial list of 10° could never be corrected and it steadily increased. All power and lighting were lost in the after half of the ship, and as the damage control parties explored with flashlights, they found compartment after compartment flooding.

In the minutes after she was hit, the ship had continued ahead on her remaining starboard shaft, but turned slowly left and soon found herself heading toward the enemy-held coast of Guadalcanal. Using the general announcing system to communicate with his remaining engine and steering gear, Kitts brought her head around toward Tulagi, but when the list reached 16° he stopped his last shaft, hoping the list could be stabilized with no way on.

Shortly after 0100, the list reached 20°, the lube oil supply failed, and the engine had to be shut down. Kitts announced on his reactivated TBS that he was preparing to abandon ship. When the list reached 23° he ordered the bridge abandoned, all engine rooms and firerooms secured, all hands topside, and life rafts and floater nets put in the water. At 0130 he ordered all hands except the salvage crew over the side.

After the excitement of the aircraft flares, Tisdale ordered *Honolulu* to sweep eastward, keeping about 15,000 yards off the Guadalcanal shore, to make sure there were no unaccounted for Japanese still there. At 0130 *Honolulu*'s SG showed eight ships on the screen—Tisdale wasn't sure how many were friendly. A moment later, *New Orleans* reported a submarine on the surface. Perhaps the other cruisers had been hit by submarine torpedoes. At 0139 he ordered *Honolulu* to clear Iron Bottom Bay to the west and then head south. As his flagship squared away on her westerly course, *Fletcher* and *Drayton* came out of the black and fell in astern.

Half an hour earlier *Northampton* had announced over TBS that she was preparing to abandon ship, so Tisdale told Hayler to set course to pass close aboard. As he approached the still flaming wreck at high speed, life rafts and groups of men were suddenly sighted in the oily water dead ahead. Hayler brought *Hono-*

lulu hard right and slowed to keep from capsizing the rafts. As he passed, Tisdale directed *Fletcher* and *Drayton* to pick up the men in the water and stand by *Northampton,* but he instructed Hayler to continue at 30 knots. Enough American cruisers had been hit that night.

By 0200 *Northampton* was nearing the end. The fires aft and on the boat deck could no longer be contained and the pressure on the firemain was falling. *Fletcher* and *Drayton* were hauling men out of the water as fast as they went in. At 0240 the list had reached 35° and Captain Kitts saw the situation was hopeless. He ordered the salvage party over the side and followed them into the water. At 0304 *Northampton* rolled over to port and sank stern first, her bow reaching 60° toward the sky as she slid under.

After they had cleared to the east, ComDesDiv 9 in *Lamson* directed *Lardner* to join and the two ships patrolled to the southeast awaiting orders. About 0130 he received instructions, relayed through Guadalcanal, to assist *Minneapolis,* reported to be proceeding toward Lunga Point. Not finding her there, he searched north toward Tulagi and finally made contact with the damaged cruiser at 0254. She was moving slowly but steadily toward Tulagi, so the two ships screened her as she limped along.

As dawn broke, *Maury* went alongside *New Orleans* in the outer reaches of Tulagi Harbor and dropped her hook to anchor the two ships—the big ship had lost her anchors with her bow. A bit later *Minneapolis* crept in with the salvage tug *Bobolink* alongside. She was taken well into the inner harbor, moored against the beach to coconut trees and quickly covered with camouflage nets. Later in the morning, *New Orleans,* with *Maury* alongside as a tug, was moved even deeper into the jungle, up McFarland Creek alongside the PT boat tender *Jamestown,* and was similarly camouflaged. *Pensacola* rode at anchor in the bay behind Tulagi Harbor; her crew, augmented by personnel from the growing naval base, was already busily working to patch her up and pump her out.

With daylight, Tisdale returned to Iron Bottom Bay, searched the area for any remaining enemy, then headed for Tulagi. As soon as *Honolulu* was in visual contact with *Minneapolis,* Wright directed Tisdale to take *Lamson* and *Lardner* and proceed to Espiritu. *Fletcher* with 646 *Northampton* survivors and *Drayton* with 127 had already cleared Lengo Channel on their way south.

In the following frantic days the three damaged cruisers were safely escorted to Espiritu for temporary repairs and ultimately back to the States to be rebuilt. All three rejoined the fleet before the war ended.

USS New Orleans *(CA-32), with bow blown off back to turret two, Tulagi Harbor, 1 December 1942. Photo from U.S. Naval Institute.*

USS Minneapolis *(CA-36), just after entering Tulagi Harbor, 1 December 1942. Photo from National Archives.*

USS Minneapolis *(CA-36), closeup of damaged bow, Tulagi Harbor, 1 December 1942. Photo from National Archives.*

USS Minneapolis *(CA-36), emergency repairs to bow using coconut logs, Tulagi Harbor, December 1942. Photo from National Archives.*

USS Minneapolis *(CA-36), rigging camouflage nets; USS Bobolink (ATF-5) alongside. Tulagi Harbor, December 1942. Photo from U.S. Naval Institute.*

USS Minneapolis *(CA-36), camouflaged and moored to the beach, Tulagi Harbor, December 1942. Photo from U.S. Naval Institute.*

USS Minneapolis *(CA-36), at Espiritu Santo, New Hebrides, fitted with temporary bow for voyage back to the United States, January 1943. Photo from Naval Historical Center*

Tulagi, 1 December 1942. PT boat loaded with Northampton survivors approaches Pensacola; New Orleans, with Maury alongside as tug, at left, moving towards McFarland Creek. Florida Island in background. Official U.S. Navy photo

USS New Orleans *(CA-32), with temporary repairs, on the way back to the States for permanent repairs. Photo from U.S. Naval Institute.*

USS Pensacola *(CA-24), alongside USS Vestal (AR-4), receiving temporary repairs, Espiritu Santo, New Hebrides, 17 December 1942. Photo from National Archives.*

USS Honolulu *(CL-48) off Mare Island, 26 October 1942. Photo from National Archives.*

❦ IV ❧
THE REPORT

Uaited States Navy Regulations require all commanders to prepare action reports of any engagement with an enemy. Men who had expended every ounce of their human energy in the preparation and conduct of the battle, who had lived unending hours of anxiety, tension, and even terror, who had seen their plans, their hopes, and beliefs proved faulty and their comrades and their beautiful ships destroyed, had to sit down and try to report what had happened. As the guns roared and the ships shook, the human participants performed the actions for which they were trained, or stared in fascination. They did not jot things down and record the time.

It was Wright's duty to keep his superiors informed so they could continue to pursue the larger struggle. Immediately after giving his order to commence firing, he had transmitted in plain language to ComSoPac, "Am engaging enemy surface forces." Five hours after the first shot he amplified to Halsey,

From CTF 67 to COMSOPAC, Time 301730 Z:
COMTASKFOR 67 REPORTS OPENED FIRE ON 4 SHIPS BELIEVED TRANSPORTS AT CAPE ESPERANCE. HITS AND FIRES WERE SEEN. SIX MINUTES LATER 3 AND PERHAPS 4 HEAVY CRUISERS STRUCK BY TORPEDOES BELIEVED FIRED BY DESTROYERS AND SUBMA-RINES. SINCE THEN HAVE BEEN UNABLE TO COMMUNICATE WITH OTHER SHIPS. NORTHAMPTON BURNED TOTAL LOSS. BELIEVE PENSACOLA SAME. NEW ORLEANS PROCEEDING TO

TULAGI 5 KNOTS. MINNEAPOLIS SAME WITH BOW BLOWN OFF
THREE FIREROOMS FLOODED. BELIEVE HONOLULU ALL RIGHT.
NO INFORMATION OF DESTROYERS.

Almost seven hours later he sent,

From CTF 67 to COMSOPAC, Time 302350 Z:
AT TULAGI ARE FOLLOWING: PENSACOLA TORPEDO HIT AND
SEVERE FIRE AFT. NEW ORLEANS WITH BOW BLOWN OFF TO
NUMBER TWO TURRET. PERKINS, MAURY ASSISTING ABOVE
SHIPS UNDAMAGED. MINNEAPOLIS AS PREVIOUSLY REPORTED.
LARDNER AND LAMSON WITH TISDALE AND UNDAMAGED. NO
FURTHER WORD OF NORTHAMPTON. FLETCHER AND DRAY-
TON REPORTED SEPARATELY BY FLETCHER. ONE JAPANESE
CRUISER SEEN TO BLOW UP AND IT IS KNOWN ADDITIONAL
JAPANESE SHIPS WERE DESTROYED AS WELL AS OTHERS DAM-
AGED. AM COLLECTING DATA.

He then outlined his limited capability to receive and decode messages.
A few hours later, after he had conferred with the captains of the ships that
were with him at Tulagi, he amplified to ComSoPac with,

BELIEVE DAMAGE TO ENEMY AS FOLLOWS: 4 DESTROYERS TWO
CRUISERS TWO AFIRM PREP ONE AFIRM KING SUNK. TWO AFIRM
PREP DAMAGED. ONE CRUISER AND FIVE DESTROYERS ESCAPED
UNDAMAGED. ESTIMATE ENEMY FORCE CONSISTED OF NINE
DESTROYERS FIVE TRANSPORTS OR CARGO SHIPS THREE CRUIS-
ERS. ENEMY GUNFIRE UNIMPRESSIVE. SAIL GEORGE RADARS OF
GREAT BENEFIT.

He could do no more.
In the following days he collected information from every source available
to understand and describe the events that occurred off Tassafaronga. He had
actually observed little of the enemy or his actions and he was blinded at a critical
moment when his flagship exploded. He didn't even know what his subordinate
commanders had said to each other over the TBS during the agonizing silence

while his own TBS was out. He would have to wait until his captains had time to prepare their reports to him before he would be able to make a sensible report to Halsey. He was sure that he did not fully comprehend what had happened.

There were basic questions that had to be answered. What Japanese ships were present during the battle? What were their probable movements? What losses had they sustained? He assembled the information which had been available to him prior to, during, and after the battle. He methodically listed it as follows:

SOURCE	INFORMATION
Coastwatcher	Ten destroyers departed in a southeasterly direction from the Buin-Faisi area before noon November 30.
Coastwatcher	Two cruisers and three destroyers arrived Buin-Faisi area from southeast, December 1.
Guadalcanal air	Evening search 30 November—no sightings. Morning search 1 December 1 CV 1 CL at 0820 250 miles from Guadalcanal course 300 speed 25.
S.G. Radars	At least eight vessels in the group which was originally picked up at 2306. Some large and some small vessels in the group.
Pilot of cruiser plane	Several large and some small vessels in the group at which our cruisers first fired. At the same time there was an additional group of five or six destroyers about four or five miles distant from first group and closer to Tassafaronga. When first sighted these destroyers were on a south-easterly course but when firing started they took up northwesterly course and radically increased speed.
FLETCHER, DRAYTON	Reports of bearings and distances of targets when torpedoes were fired indicates that these two destroyers fired at targets four or five miles apart.
PERKINS	Saw gun flashes from three or four enemy vessels farther to the left (east) than the group of five at which we fired torpedoes.
Cruiser reports	Our two rear (eastern) cruisers definitely identify their targets as destroyers. *Pensacola* and *New*

	Orleans identified cruisers as *Mogami* or *Yubari*. *Minneapolis* identified one target as destroyer.
MINNEAPOLIS Observer	At about 2328 three enemy ships had reached a position on the port beam of our cruisers and about 6,000 yards away. At this time targets at which *Minneapolis* was shooting were at least three miles westward of these ships.
Various	At about 2328 at least three torpedoes struck *Minneapolis* and *New Orleans.* These came from port (south). At about the same time three torpedoes were seen to cross through destroyer formation from port to starboard. Our destroyers were then about three miles ahead of our cruisers. After *New Orleans* was hit and had turned to port another torpedo came from ahead and passed close alongside.
PENSACOLA, NORTHAMPTON	The torpedoes which struck *Pensacola* and *Northampton* came from the west. These ships were hit about 10 and 20 minutes, respectively, later than the *Minneapolis.*
DRAYTON	The *Drayton* at 2346 observed and tracked three enemy ships near Cape Esperance.
Cruiser plane pilot	At about midnight there were two large ships well to the west of the battle scene. One of these was standing to the Northwest at very high speed. The other was following a few miles astern at lower speed and smoking heavily.
Various	After 2345, when gunfire had ceased, no Japanese vessels could be found on any radar screen, although all radars were then being used for searching.
MINNEAPOLIS	Enemy light cruiser on fire and burning vigorously a few miles to the Southwest. Heavy tripod structure distinctly seen. Two other Japanese vessels seen to be burning after gunfire ceased. One exploded. One sank. Later passed close alongside

	capsized Japanese vessel with broken back. Visible part of keel variously estimated as 300 to 500 feet. Enemy held section of shore was clearly seen after moon rose and there were no ships in vicinity and no activity on the beach.
NORTHAMPTON	A reliable and experienced chief petty officer, while in a liferaft southeast of Savo Island, saw submarine emerge a short distance to the west, turn on identification lights (one green over one white) and then submerge.
Intelligence report	One submarine arrived at Kakimbo at 1230 on 30 November.
PERKINS	Saw ship at distance of 4,000 yards explode when hit by one of our torpedoes.
Various	The target at which we were shooting suddenly disappeared from radar screen.
MINNEAPOLIS	Sank first target taken under fire; shifted fire to second target. Damaged this vessel.
NEW ORLEANS	First target, a destroyer, fired on by *New Orleans* and others. Target sank. Second target, light cruiser, possibly a heavy. Two other ships had been firing on this target but had stopped. Target seen to sink while *New Orleans* was firing at it. Third target was a large ship, probably an AK. Fired on by *New Orleans* and several others. Blew up violently. Saw two other destroyers sunk by fire of other vessels.
PENSACOLA	Early in the action saw a *Mogami* or *Yubari* class cruiser very heavily hit—sure it sank. Saw one other cruiser badly damaged.
NORTHAMPTON	Saw a destroyer on fire shortly after our other cruisers opened fire. Our third salvo landed directly on a destroyer and sank it. Shifted to another destroyer and it caught fire and vanished.
HONOLULU	Fired on two destroyers and saw them sink.
MAURY	Saw one Japanese ship burning during gun action.

	Saw *Honolulu* hitting one ship heavily. Saw one ship break in two and sink.
LARDNER	A few minutes after our cruisers started firing, saw three Japanese ships somewhat to the east of ships at which our first cruisers fired. These three ships seemed to be still heading to the east, but the others had stopped or turned west.

As soon as he had done all he could to ensure the safety of his ships at Tulagi, Admiral Wright and his staff had been transported to Lunga Point by PT boat and were soon on their way by air to Espiritu, where he shifted his flag to his one remaining cruiser, *Honolulu.* This also had the advantage of being with Tisdale so the two could work together to figure out what had happened. As soon as immediate emergencies were taken care of and they had gotten enough sleep to think clearly, Admiral Wright called his staff together and started on his action report. While waiting for the reports of his subordinates, he could organize his thoughts and have his assistants collect the messages and other data pertinent to his analysis. As soon as he received each ship's action report, he studied it in detail and compared the reported events and observations with those reported by others. His understanding of the action and what had actually transpired grew with each scrap of information.

Though words are helpful in describing events, pictures are often better. *Fletcher*'s Track Chart, Figure 1, was the clearest picture of the battle submitted by any of Wright's subordinates. It showed a total of five enemy ships on a southeasterly course, close to the Guadalcanal shore. It also showed the track of the lead destroyers as they raced around Savo and swept southward to probe the sound. Although *Minneapolis* was permanently knocked out of the battle at an early stage, her SG radar was not. Lieutenant E. C. Callahan, her radar officer, had it back on the line shortly after the explosions and observed the remainder of the action from an excellent vantage point. His detailed report was enclosed as a part of Captain Rosendahl's report and was the basis for many of Rosendahl's conclusions. Callahan's charts of the battle are shown in Figures 2 and 3. They show a total of six enemy ships on Chart I, but only five are accounted for on Chart II.

Admiral Wright completed his Herculean task and forwarded his thick action report to ComSoPac by courier on the 9th of December. It enclosed copies of the action reports of each of his subordinate commanders and the CO of each of the ships which had participated in the battle. He had started by describing the organization of his task force and the events which led up to the engagement. Step by step he reviewed the messages received, the plans he had prepared, the instructions he had issued to his subordinates, and a chronology of the actions he had taken. He had a track chart prepared to show his approach to the battle area and the maneuvers of his tactical units during the battle. He presented a chronological narrative of the engagement as seen by himself and his subordinates. He outlined the movements of all of the units under his command after the action and he reported the damage suffered by his own ships. The portion of his report dealing with the enemy bears quoting in full.

ENEMY FORCE—COMPOSITION AND MOVEMENTS

27. All attempts to determine with certainty the composition of the Japanese forces participating in the action, or the tactics employed by those forces, or the damage sustained by the enemy, are defeated by conditions preventing accurate observation. The night was very dark, with sky completely overcast. Surface visibility was less than 4,000 yards, and the range to enemy surface vessels was at no time less than 6,000 yards. During the approach, the firing of our torpedoes, and the opening stages of the gun action no enemy ships were seen. Thereafter individual ships were seen, for brief intervals only, when illuminated by star shells or the loom of burning ships. In addition, no individual who did see anything could also note and record the time of the occurrence. As a result the recordings of times in all the reports are subject to suspicion.

28. In attempting to visualize the action and to comprehend the difficulties in the way of any observer's following the developments of the battle, it will be helpful to recall that the S.G. radars are capable of giving either a general view of objects in the vicinity of the observing ship, or an accurate bearing and distance of any one object, but that the two functions cannot be performed simultaneously. Since the S.G. radars were necessarily concentrated for considerable intervals on obtaining bearing and range of own ship's target, there was no continuity in the observation of the very rapidly changing situations.

29. Attempts to analyze the torpedo attack which disabled the *Minneapolis* and *New Orleans* have proven particularly baffling. The number of torpedoes involved (at least three struck the two cruisers and at least three passed through our van destroyer formation at about the same time) and the wide spread (two cruisers, one thousand yards apart, struck simultaneously, and other torpedo wakes crossing three or four thousand yards ahead of cruiser positions) seem to rule out the possibility of attack by a single submarine at this time; the observed positions of the enemy surface vessels before and during the gun action makes it seem improbable that torpedoes with speed-distance characteristics similar to our own could have reached the cruisers at the time they did if launched from any of the enemy destroyers or cruisers which were observed to be present.

30. The Brief of Available Information will show how little is really known about the enemy forces participating in the action, or what their movements were, or what damage they suffered.

31. About the best we can do under the circumstances is to make those assumptions which seem most logical and which are not in conflict with such evidence as is available. Upon that basis the following opinions are ventured:

    (a) That at about 2315 Japanese surface units were under way between Cape Esperance and Tassafaronga on a southeasterly course at about 17 knots, approaching enemy-held parts of Guadalcanal Island for the purpose of landing supplics and/or troops.

    (b) That Japanese submarines may have been present, stationed approximately on the line Tassafaronga–Savo Island.

    (c) That the Japanese surface force was operating in at least two groups, the leading, or easternmost group, consisting of five or six destroyers and the rear group of about four cruisers and about four or five destroyers.

    (d) That noncombatant Japanese ships were probably not present.

    (e) That the presence of our task force was probably not known, at least until shortly before we opened fire.

    (f) That at about the time we opened fire the cruisers turned to the northward, and that when two were heavily hit the others escaped to the northwestward.

(g)   That most, if not all, of the destroyers stood in to make a torpedo attack on our cruisers, and that at least three survived to reach torpedo firing position.

(h)   That the *Minneapolis* and *New Orleans* were disabled by torpedoes, probably fired by destroyers.

(i)   That undetermined vessels to the westward of our position, perhaps cruisers trying to escape, or perhaps a submarine or submarines fortunately placed, fired long range torpedo shots which hit the *Pensacola* and *Northampton* merely through luck, since the maneuvers of those vessels in clearing our damaged ships could not have been predicted when the torpedoes were fired.

(j)   That no supplies or troops were landed on the northern shore of Guadalcanal, although some personnel probably reached there by swimming.

(k)   That probable Japanese losses are two light cruisers and seven destroyers.

PERFORMANCE OF OWN FORCES

32.   Our destroyer torpedoes were fired at such ranges that it is improbable that they were very effective. I fully approve of the action of the Commanding Officers of *Maury, Lamson,* and *Lardner* in not firing torpedoes when target had not been identified and tracked by radar. (These ships have no S.G. radars.) I also approve of the action of the Commanding Officer *Drayton* in firing only two torpedoes at one target and four at another, since results of his radar tracking failed to demonstrate that suitable targets were within effective range.

33.   The gunnery performance of our cruisers was excellent. The volume of fire was very impressive and great havoc was raised with the enemy ships. I doubt that any of the groups taken under fire escaped, with the exception of two cruisers which apparently made an undetected turn to the northwestward when other cruisers were being hit. A very high standard of gunnery proficiency was necessary to get results under the conditions obtaining, since it was necessary to depend largely upon radar information for ranging, pointing and spotting. Star shells appeared to function fairly well, but smoke caused great interference with vision even when star shells were advantageously placed.

He followed these key paragraphs with several under the title of "Performance of Personnel" in which he reported "the performance of our officers and enlisted personnel left nothing to be desired," approved "without reservation all the actions" of Admiral Tisdale, absolved the commanding officers of the four damaged cruisers "from any blame for the torpedoing of their ships," complimented the crews of the damaged ships for successfully bringing their charges safely to port, and spoke highly of the resolute efforts of the crew of *Northampton* in the futile struggle to save their ship and the skill of the skippers of *Fletcher* and *Drayton* in saving so many of the survivors.

He then commented on the effectiveness of communications with particular emphasis on the vulnerability and limitations of the TBS. He reported satisfactory use of recognition lights and suggested battery-powered units be used in emergencies. He went into detail reporting the numerous material failures in the radio communication system and made recommendations for improvement.

With respect to radar, he had high praise for the SG, but emphasized the need for repeaters since its picture and information was needed simultaneously at all levels of command and throughout the weapon systems. He was much less complimentary about the FC gunnery radar, particularly with respect to spotting. He added emphatically that a separate recognition-type radar was a must for night fighting.

As for cruiser aircraft, he related the sorry performance of his SOCs in not arriving in time to be useful and the mistaken observation that resulted in dropping of a flare over a beached wreck. To summarize, he said

48. Our planes in this case had no influence upon the course of the action, but the presence of gasoline in *Minneapolis* and *New Orleans* seriously endangered those vessels. I am still of the opinion that, for the types of operations that our 10,000 ton cruisers have thus far experienced in the South Pacific area, the price we pay for planes, in fire hazard, excess weights, and loss of desirable positions for AA weapons, is very greatly in excess of the value received.

He continued with paragraphs on the possibility of using mines along the coast of Guadalcanal, recommendations with respect to approach routes to Guadalcanal, navigation problems and the need for better navigational information of the area. A remarkable section then follows, beginning with

Figure 1. *USS Fletcher's Track Chart.*

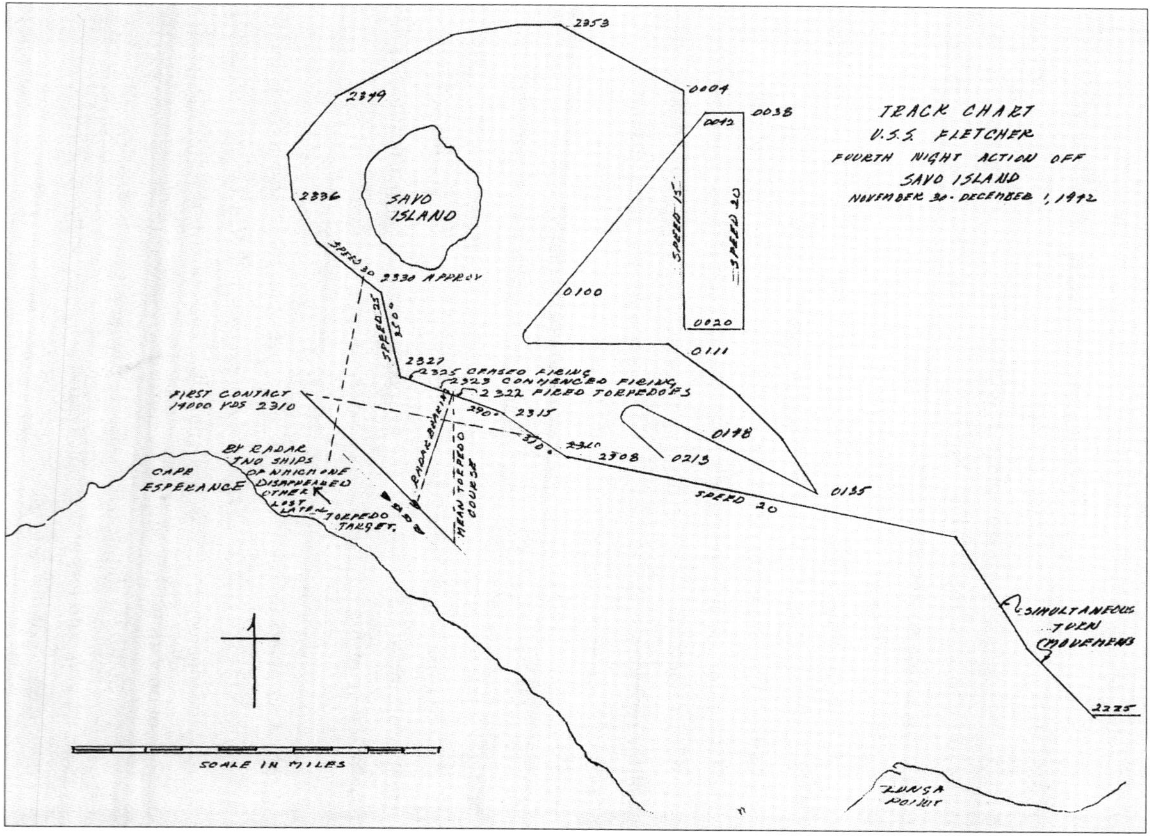

Figure 2. *Lieutenant Callahan's Chart I.*

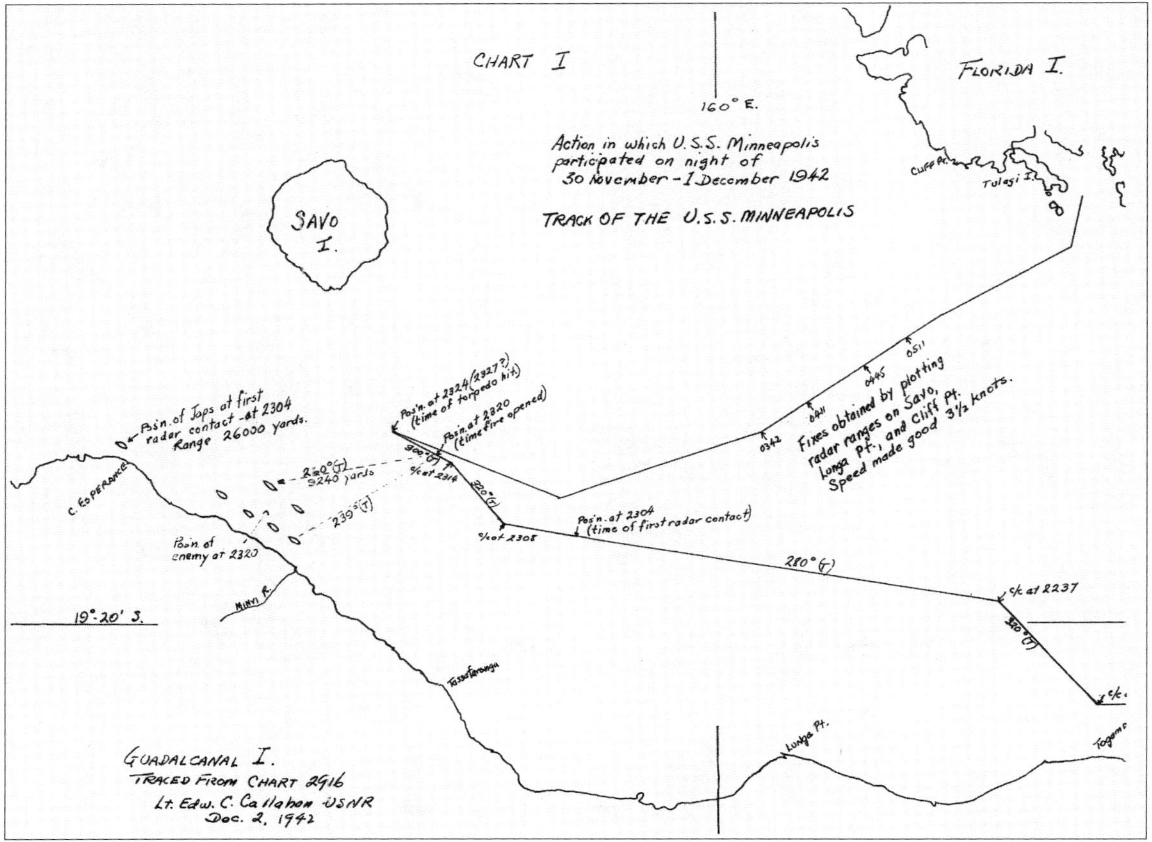

Figure 3. *Lieutenant Callahan's Chart II.*

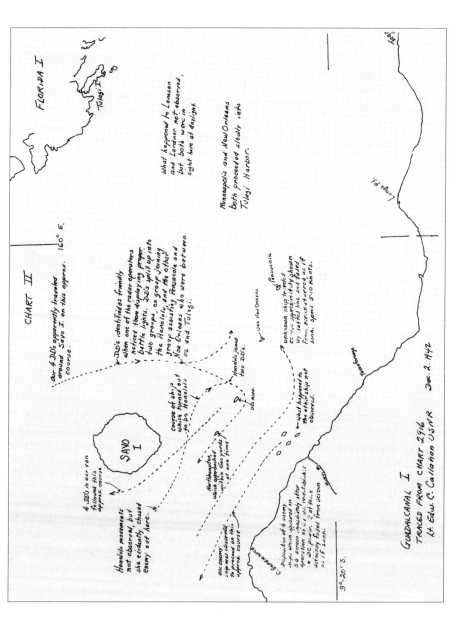

SUITABILITY OF CRUISER TYPES FOR NIGHT ACTION

53. The volume and accuracy of fire of the *Honolulu* was tremendously impressive. For the types of night action in which our cruisers have engaged in the various battles near Savo Island I consider one 10,000-ton, 6-inch cruiser to be the equivalent of at least two of our 10,000-ton, 8-inch ships.

He then refers to the following section of Admiral Tisdale's Action Report:

12. The fact that the *Honolulu,* the only 10,000-ton, 6-inch gun cruiser in the column was the only cruiser not torpedoed might at first be ascribed to the fortunes of war. But the fact that *Helena* received only minor damage in two previous night engagements indicates that the type of ship may have some bearing on its value at night in comparison with heavy cruisers. That the *Boise* was damaged during the second Savo might appear to explode this theory. It is understood that the *Boise* used search lights, that the *Helena* used no illumination; that the *Honolulu* used stars. These ships are veritably ablaze when their main battery is firing so the Commander Task Unit Sixty-Seven Point Two Point Three doubts that the damage or non-damage can be based too heavily upon the method of illumination used during actual firing. It also is doubtful if the results can be called all luck or coincidence. Nor can it be assumed that the light cruiser captains are necessarily better seamen than the heavy cruiser captains or the crews better trained. But there are two factors that will bear careful analysis in the cases mentioned: first, the built-in ability of this type to fire accurately while maneuvering; second, fire power. The reports of the *Boise* and *Helena* are not available to me for study. The thought is offered for what it may be worth.

Wright added

I do not know the answer.

He concluded his voluminous report with a plea for more time for training, particularly gunnery exercises, and for unit integrity so that a team spirit can be developed among commanders and crews can become accustomed to working with each other.

Ten days later he added a memorandum containing the following supplementary information:

(a) Searchlights were not used by any of our vessels.

(b) Believe no searchlights were used by Japanese. The few Japanese star shells seen had the same greenish tinge that has been commented upon before.

(c) The only searchlight that I saw at any time was the one on shore at Lunga Point. It was a very good light visible for many miles. I believe that this searchlight was the one sighted by *Honolulu* when she was to the northeast of Savo Island at about 0015.

(d) I believe that the supposed destroyer attack on the *New Orleans,* made some time after she was torpedoed (at about 2335?), was not an actual attack, but that she sighted and fired at the *Lardner.* I personally saw one of our ships, which I believed to be the *New Orleans,* firing 40mm to the northeastward at this time. The *Lardner* reports that 40mm were fired at her (tracers of 40mm are easily recognized).

(e) Although the torpedoes caused fires on each of our heavy cruisers, I believe that practically the only material which burned was gasoline, fuel oil and diesel oil. Ammunition exploded in *Pensacola* and *Northampton* from the heat of the intense fires. The types of fires which have been so disastrous in the past—paint, bedding, clothing, and miscellaneous combustibles—did not occur in any ship.

He concluded in recommending there be no relaxation in the CinCPac very strict instructions concerning combustibles.

Carleton Wright knew that his days in command of his task force were numbered. Although he believed his guns had inflicted heavy damage on the enemy in exchange for his four cruisers out of action, he could not prove it. With minor deviations he had fought the action just as his past experience and best judgment told him to, but his force had been shattered and such losses were intolerable. His report would be his swan song, but he had to rush it forward because the information it contained might prevent future catastrophes. Though he did not know where he had failed, or why, he forwarded his report and prepared to step off the center stage of the Pacific war.

⸺ V ⸺

THE ENDORSEMENTS

On the 13th of December, the Commander South Pacific Force, Admiral William F. Halsey Jr., forwarded an advance copy of Admiral Wright's report to the Commander in Chief, Pacific Fleet, Admiral Chester W. Nimitz. He had just received it that day and forwarded it without comment; his full review and endorsement would follow later.

Admiral Nimitz forwarded his report, which enclosed Admiral Wright's report, to the Commander in Chief, U.S. Fleet, Admiral Ernest J. King, on 15 February 1943. He had the advantage of hindsight, which included important events in the months of December and January, and he had the benefit of intelligence resources not available to CTF 67 when he prepared his report. His first four paragraphs were

1. On the night of 30 November 1942, the Japanese were turned back in their first important attempt to reinforce Guadalcanal since the decisive engagements of mid-November. Task Force 67 under Rear Admiral C. H. Wright attacked before the landing could be accomplished, and at severe cost to our ships, forced the enemy to withdraw. This action, following the defeats of a fortnight earlier, apparently persuaded the Japanese to relinquish temporarily any hope of important reinforcements of Guadalcanal and to restrict themselves to small-scale supply by submarines or occasionally destroyers while building airfields for support of the route to Guadalcanal.

2. Task Force 67 inflicted this damage on the enemy:
   SUNK—4 DD (*Takanami* and 3 others)
   DAMAGED—2 more DD

3. Our own losses were:
   SUNK—*Northampton*
   SERIOUSLY DAMAGED—*Pensacola, New Orleans, Minneapolis*
   Nineteen officers and 398 men killed or missing

4. It is not clear what enemy forces were at the scene of action. The best information from intelligence sources is 8 DD, of which 6 were acting as transports. There were also believed to be both large and midget SS in the area. It will be noted in the narrative, based on ship reports, that there is mention of damage to enemy cruisers and auxiliaries or transports. Because of conflicting intelligence information, it has been assumed that these were in fact enemy destroyers.

These paragraphs were followed by sections which traced the background and events leading up to the battle in less detail than we have already covered above, then continued with the following:

24. Commander Task Force 67 did not receive any contacts to supplement the original intelligence received from Commander South Pacific Force. All aircraft searches on 30 November, including special ones out of Guadalcanal, failed to locate any approaching enemy ships despite good weather and 100% coverage of search sectors. His additional information for the 30th was the negative search report, a coastwatcher's report of the departure of 12 destroyers from Buin the night of the 29th, and a despatch from Commander South Pacific Force that the enemy force might contain only destroyers.

25. It is still not known what enemy ships were actually present during the engagement. Any estimate, such as that given in paragraph 4, must be based for the present on the following information, most of it not available to Commander Task Force 67 on the night of 30 November.

   (a) Buin-Faisi coast watcher reported that 12 DD departed from their anchorages on the night of 29–30 November. This was the maximum number of destroyers sighted in the Buin area for some time. There is no record of where they were on 30 November; they could have been outside our search to the east or west or concealed in harbors enroute to Guadalcanal.

(b) One of our search planes at about 1300, 30 November, sighted 6 DD in Tonolei and 11 AK in the area. These DD could have reached Tassafaronga that night by departing after the search plane was clear.

(c) On 30 November there was a DF bearing, possibly of Eighth Fleet Commander, just east of Buin, indicating the possible presence of forces at sea in readiness either to go into Guadalcanal that night or to support at a distance.

(d) Late on the 30th a large XAV[1] (First reported as a CV[2]) arrived at Tonolei with 5 DD.

(e) The action off Savo Island was fought close to the Japanese controlled coast; it may be presumed that many Japanese survivors reached the friendly shore. The only prisoners of war picked up declared they were from the destroyer *Takanami,* one of 5 DD [later changed to 7] bringing supplies, and that no other ships were present. Later it was disclosed that 3 of the prisoners were from the destroyer *Kikutsuki* which they stated was 1 of 8–10 destroyers present carrying supplies. (The *Kikutsuki* is listed in several captured documents as sunk at Tulagi on 4 May 1942.)

(f) It has been the custom for Japanese forces to approach in separate groups. The evidence is strong that on the night of 30 November there were three groups of Japanese ships off Savo Island, the center one of 7 ships being the only one picked up by S.G. radar.

(g) Some observers on our ships and one in the water specifically claim to have seen cruisers and transports.

(h) On 1 December the only ships retiring from Guadalcanal sighted by our search planes were 1 CV and 1 DD 250 miles distant at 0823.

(i) At daylight on 2 December, by coast watcher report, there were 9 DD with various AO and AK in the Buin area.

1   Converted seaplane tender
2   Aircraft carrier

(j)   The next morning there were 18 DD, 11 of which departed to the southeast. Later in the day 3 CA entered the port, remained a few hours, and departed to the eastward.

CinCPac's report continued with a narrative of the action in less detail than we have covered above from the individual ship reports and then concluded with

COMMENTS AND CONCLUSIONS

54.   It is undesirable to operate heavy ships in confined waters such as Savo Sound [Iron Bottom Bay] unless such ships are the only ones available to counter important enemy threats. Not only are they in an unfavorable position for enemy torpedo attacks, but effectiveness of radar is so reduced that our present invaluable superiority in this device may be lost. In this particular action, lack of early information on enemy movements probably required Commander South Pacific Force to direct Commander Task Force 67 to pass though Lengo Channel to arrive south of Savo Island at a definite hour. Otherwise it would have been preferable for the force to approach to the westward of Guadalcanal and to intercept north of Savo Island, in the area where the enemy is believed to station a light support screen for operations such as this. With the striking force of destroyers and PT boats now based at Tulagi, interception of the enemy at the place of our choosing should be practicable and less costly in cruiser damage.

55.   Air search out of Guadalcanal and Button[3] has failed to furnish consistent information on enemy vessels enroute to and from Guadalcanal. Having determined the times and limits of our search, the Japanese direct their movements to avoid it by routes north of Choiseul, directly down New Georgia Sound, and south of New Georgia (and probably by clever use of concealed anchorages). They have been able to reach and retire from Guadalcanal without being detected by aircraft. With increased base facilities at Guadalcanal-Tulagi, and establishment of B-17 and PBY search there, it should be possible to improve the effectiveness of our search.

---

3   Espiritu Santo

56. Immediately on contact the Task Force Commander put into effect Radar Condition One (no restriction on the use of radar). This desirable procedure should be followed in all engagements.

57. This action emphasizes the urgent need for flashless powder for all large caliber guns. No hostile ship got closer to our force than 4,000–6,000 yards and none was seen except by star shell illumination or when hit and afire. Yet probably by following the flashes from our gunfire the enemy was able to track our formation and fire an effective spread of torpedoes. Small quantities of flashless powder pellets have been received over a period of several months; production needs to be accelerated.

58. The Japanese took advantage of the land background of Guadalcanal, which reduced the efficiency of both radar and visual observation from our ships. Commander Task Force 67's operation plan provided for flare illumination by planes to counteract this advantage held by the enemy. However, because of light winds the planes were delayed in taking off from Tulagi at the appointed hour. As a result they did not arrive over the battle area until most of the fighting had ceased. One of the planes, mistaking a beached hulk for an enemy ship underway, reported it as such and was directed to drop flares. The resultant excellent illumination discomfited our nearby damaged ships which were silhouetted by it.

59. Destroyers fired torpedoes at an excessive range. Torpedo firing ranges at night of more than 4,000–5,000 yards are not acceptable. Favorably disposed ahead of the cruisers, our destroyers should have found it possible to close the range to less than 4,000 yards before attacking. By firing star shells at the moment of launching torpedoes, they remove any chance of surprise.

60. S.G. radar was again invaluable both for the search and gunnery. Reflections from the land background blanked out target echoes so that few of the ships were able to pick up targets with other radars. Without this excellent radar our force would have had little knowledge of the enemy's movements. There are so many uses for S.G. radar that as soon as single installations are completed on combatant vessels, large ships should be provided with an extra set. Production of remote repeaters for the PPI search should be given high priority.

61. As a result of the very large explosion that tore off *New Orleans* bow and number 1 turret, her forward FC radar and TBS were out of commission. Other radars, including S.G., remained in operation, demonstrating that suitable shock mounting can be provided for these radars. Under such trying circumstances radars on other ships have been disabled by shock. The sturdy performance of *New Orleans's* radars is considered to be the result of efficient antishock measures prescribed by the Fleet Maintenance Office, U.S. Pacific Fleet.

62. In enclosure (A), Commander Task Force 67 recommends a number of improvements in communication material to reduce damage from shock.

63. PT Boats are admirably fitted for close inshore engagements such as this. The 16 PT Boats in Tulagi on 30 November could have supplemented the destroyer torpedo attack to good effect. They were ordered to remain in port, however, because of possibility of error in identification. This danger could have been diminished by assigning them operating and retirement areas clear of our larger ships.

64. In every night action identification of our ships has been a matter of concern and often of confusion. Our present recognition lights have been helpful but have frequently served the enemy almost as well as ourselves. Installation of infrared or radar recognition must be expedited.

65. In this action, cruiser planes had been flown off and other causes of fires in previous engagements largely eliminated. The severe fires experienced in several of the cruisers resulted from the ignition of fuel oil and gasoline by torpedo explosions.

66. The restricted waters of the Solomons-Bismark archipelago present many opportunities for offensive mining with both contact and influence types. Plans are being developed for laying fields from surface vessels and aircraft. These include the location suggested by Commander Task Force 67 along the north coast of Guadalcanal, where Japanese vessels unload supplies and reinforcements. In this action the enemy force remained very close to the beach, making visual or radar detection difficult. Mines might have been effective in countering these tactics.

67. It is noted that one factor in saving the *Minneapolis* was her electric submersible pumps and a portable gasoline-driven salvage pump received during overhaul at Pearl Harbor shortly before this action.

Self-powered salvage and fire fighting pumps might have saved a number of our ships which have sunk.

68. This action provides more examples of dangers inherent in TBS. We know from past engagements that the Japanese have picked up TBS broadcasts to their advantage. Before firing commenced on the evening of 30 November, there were several TBS communications within our force from the time of the first radar contact, including conversation between the destroyer commander and the Commander Task Force 67 concerning initiation of the torpedo attack. Some of these may have been intercepted by the enemy. Japanese prisoners state that our ships were sighted before firing commenced and that the Japanese ships deployed at once from column. Because of the visibility conditions existing, it is doubtful that the ships were sighted visually but quite likely that TBS messages were intercepted.

69. The Commander in Chief, U.S. Pacific Fleet, agrees with the remarks of Commander Task Force 67 under "Training and Organization." The rapid changes in command of Task Forces and ships and the shifting of vessels between Task Units have prevented the development sought in our peace time training of thorough indoctrination between a commander and his subordinates. In this action, for example, the 4 leading destroyers had not operated together as a unit and had no division commander present. The 2 rear destroyers left escort duty and fell in astern of Task Force 67 just before the battle. These defects result from paucity of cruisers and destroyers. Now that more ships are becoming available to the Pacific Fleet it is hoped to correct these deficiencies and to maintain reasonable continuity of organization.

70. In this connection, readiness of new destroyers joining the Fleet has been below acceptable standards. They have had little antisubmarine training, inadequate gun practices, sketchy radar training, and in some instances have never fired a torpedo. This is a situation that was forced on them because of well known circumstances and is now being remedied.

71. The enemy's most damaging weapon has been the torpedo. It appears to function well mechanically and carries a most powerful explosive charge. Destroyers and cruisers are skilled in using it. On the other hand, in no night action has our destroyers' major offensive strength,

the torpedo, been used effectively. This failure results in part from the deficiencies in destroyer operations previously mentioned; it results in large part from lack of firing individual and division torpedo practices. It is expected that Unit and Force Commanders will take opportunities for more torpedo practices by all destroyers.

72. Our torpedoes of all types are not sufficiently deadly. This important defect requires immediate attention.

73. The personnel of this force, most of them veterans of earlier engagements, lived up to the high standard they themselves have set, not only in courage and skill in fighting the enemy but in fighting fire and damage. It is believed nothing more could have been done to save the *Northampton,* and that had anything less been done, others of the damaged cruisers would have been lost.

74. The operation order for this engagement was simple and well conceived. Except for the failure of illumination planes to arrive on schedule, the TBS communications before the torpedo attack, and the long range at which the torpedo attack was delivered, the conduct of the battle was correct. Rear Admiral Wright led his force into action resolutely and intelligently and opened fire at a range that should have permitted avoiding surprise torpedo attack. When his flagship was immobilized, he transferred direction of the force to Rear Admiral Tisdale, who continued the battle and sought the enemy with determination. The fortunes of war and the restricted waters in which we were forced to bring the enemy into action caused our ships to suffer greater loss than their leadership and action merited, and prevented them from inflicting heavier damage on the enemy.

75. As in previous engagements we are made painfully aware of the Japanese skill, both in night and day action, in the use of guns and torpedoes. To date there has been no reason to doubt his energy, persistence, and courage.

76. It is obvious that each individual ship and plane in the Pacific Fleet must reach an early peak of efficiency in the use of every weapon and appliance.

77. This means training, TRAINING and M-O-R-E T-R-A-I-N-I-N-G. Each commanding officer is called upon to do his share.
   C. W. Nimitz

Copies of this report were sent to all senior officers in the Pacific Fleet.

On 20 February 1943, Admiral Halsey finally forwarded his endorsement to Admiral Wright's action report. The first portion is quoted as follows:

1. Forwarded.

2. In this night action own force of 4 CA, CL and 6 DDs under the command of Rear Admiral C. H. Wright, USN, intercepted Japanese surface units between Cape Esperance and Tassafaronga and probably defeated their attempt to land supplies and/or troops on Guadalcanal. The picture of the entire action is so confused that the exact number of enemy surface units engaged is merely a conjecture but probably consisted of about 10 DDs and perhaps 4 light cruisers. Enemy losses can only be estimated and are put at 2 CL and 7 DD.

3. Gunfire and torpedoes were used by both sides. Enemy gunfire was sporadic and ineffective, but their torpedo fire was most effective, completely immobilizing three heavy cruisers and sinking the fourth. Whether or not these torpedoes were fired from DDs or fortunately placed submarines is questionable. Own gunfire, primarily radar controlled, appears to have been accurate and deadly. Own torpedo fire is believed to have been most ineffective. No torpedo hits were observed. This ineffectiveness of own torpedoes is attributed to firing them at excessive ranges.

4. The van [lead] destroyers, after firing torpedoes, did not assist the cruisers, but turned away and retired to the northwest. This was contrary to the instructions issued the Task Force for night action included in the basic letter as enclosure F(2). Similar lack of offensive action on the part of destroyers in future actions will not be tolerated.

In the following paragraphs Admiral Halsey comments on specific parts of Wright's action report, of which the following sections are of particular interest to this discussion:

Page 5, Par. 16—The offensive action of the van [lead] destroyers was disappointing, although some unobserved torpedo hits may have been made. Radar-controlled torpedo firing is approved and encouraged, but a review of the action indicates over-hasty expenditure.

Page 6, Par.19—If the theory of a destroyer torpedo attack is accepted, this devastating attack must have been launched from well outside 6,000 yards with only gun flashes as a point of aim. The possibility of Japanese ship-borne radar cannot be overlooked. However, the success of this attack, coupled with two equally successful later attacks, points strongly to submarine activity in support of the Japanese surface force.

Thus, the senior commanders of the Pacific Fleet dealt with a battle of historic significance. It was the event that caused the Japanese to finally recognize failure and decide to withdraw their forces from Guadalcanal. It was the end of their victories and the beginning of a long series of defeats that led to surrender in Tokyo Bay, but it was also a catastrophic embarrassment to the Pacific Command.

Admiral Halsey and Admiral Nimitz, aided and abetted by their large staffs, didn't understand what had happened, yet felt they must take a firm stand to encourage better performance in the future. After exploring every aspect they could think of, they ended in heaping criticism on the only subordinate who had used his weapons to their maximum capability and who handled his ships with both skill and determination, bringing them through the long night unscathed: Commander William Marchant Cole, U.S. Naval Academy, Class of 1924, commanding USS *Fletcher,* DD 445 and Task Group 67.4, the lead destroyers.

With the power of hindsight, let us see what really happened.

⟶ VI ⟶
THE ENEMY

The Battle of Tassafaronga can trace its heritage to London. In 1921 at a diplomatic reception, the Japanese naval attaché overheard a conversation in which it was stated that the British were developing an oxygen torpedo. He immediately forwarded this exciting news to Tokyo and the Imperial naval staff initiated a program to develop a similar torpedo for the Japanese navy. The attaché's report was erroneous; no such development had yet been undertaken by the British, but they were thinking about it.

Most steam torpedoes are descended from the Whitehead torpedo and burn alcohol with air to make steam to run their engines. Obviously, if pure oxygen were substituted for air, 21 percent of which is oxygen, the amount of oxidant would be increased for the same volume by a factor of almost five and the products of combustion would be H_2O and CO_2, both of which would be absorbed by the seawater and no wake would be left. The resulting increase in energy could be utilized to increase speed, range, or both. It was a concept easy to understand, but hard to execute. Most navies which develop their own torpedoes have experimented with oxygen torpedoes.

The Washington Naval Conference in 1921 limited the Japanese navy to three-fifths the number of capital ships and other forces possessed by the British and the American navies. Japan had been dreaming of domination of East Asia since the victory of Admiral Togo in the Russo-Japanese War, and this limitation put them at a severe disadvantage with respect to their most obvious opponent in the Pacific, the United States. The naval staff decided to concentrate on quality if they were to be denied quantity, and it allocated tremendous sums to the development of new and improved weapons. Torpedoes being the most effective weapon with which to sink ships, it was decided to concentrate on torpedoes and the craft which employed them.

But the development of an oxygen torpedo was not to be easy. Experiments began to reveal the difficulties of utilizing pure oxygen. The flame was too hot; valves, pipes, and combustors burned through; explosions occurred. The initial experimental models were found too difficult to use and too unreliable to be the basis for naval planning, so in 1926 the development was dropped.

But events around the world were progressing and Japan was making plans to extend the footholds gained from the Sino-Japanese War, originally in Manchuria and eventually southward to Shanghai. The U.S. Navy had developed huge dirigibles for long-range reconnaissance and was refining the aircraft carrier. The U.S. Fleet would be particularly difficult to approach and attack in daylight and clear weather. It was decided that the Imperial Japanese Navy would adopt a policy of fighting at night. Torpedoes would be a most important weapon with which to support this new policy, so in 1928 the oxygen torpedo program was revived. The *Fubuki* destroyer program was initiated and all cruiser classes were modified to employ these new weapons.

The key technical developments which led to a successful oxygen torpedo were the decision to initiate combustion using normal air and gradually shifting to pure oxygen, and the introduction of seawater into the combustion chamber to create steam directly and keep the combustion chamber cool enough to survive.

The first successful oxygen torpedo was the experimental Type 93 Model 1, which was demonstrated in trials in 1933. Small modifications were made to improve it and in 1936 full production was started on the torpedo used by destroyers and cruisers throughout World War II. Twenty-five feet long, two feet in diameter and weighing nearly two tons, this weapon had the following characteristics:

MODEL 1, MODIFICATION 1

Speed	*Range*
49 knots	22,000 yards
40 knots	35,000 yards
36 knots	44,000 yards

Explosive Charge—1,078 lbs

Not only did the *Fubuki*s and later destroyers carry multiple mounts from which to fire these lethal monsters, most of them were provided with 100 percent replacement torpedoes and handling systems so that after the first salvo had emptied the tubes, they could be reloaded in about 20 minutes for a second full salvo.

Such a torpedo is so inconsistent with traditional naval thinking that we might pause to reflect upon torpedoes and their use. Basically, a conventional torpedo is a weapon that is launched to run on a straight pre-set course at a pre-set depth; when it strikes the hull of a target ship, the exploder sets off the warhead, blowing a hole in the ship. Because of the high density of water as compared to air, an underwater explosion, even close to the hull of a ship, does immensely more structural damage than an equal explosion in the air. As the veteran torpedo plane pilots used to say, "If you want to fill 'em with smoke, use bombs; if you want to fill 'em with water, use torpedoes."

Conventional steam torpedoes had a top speed of about 45 knots and left a very visible wake as the nitrogen left over from the combustion air bubbled to the surface. This giveaway was satisfactory for use against slow-moving ships at short ranges, but a warship, sighting a torpedo wake at sufficient distance, had the speed and maneuverability to avoid it. Electric propulsion for torpedoes would eliminate the wake, but limited by the battery power available, they were slow and of very short range.

The Japanese Type 93, soon dubbed the Long Lance, so outperformed competitors with its extremely high speed, unbelievable range, and almost complete lack of a visible wake, that all factors in the torpedo equation have to be re-examined. It was certainly spectacular, but was it useful?

Because the wake of a steam torpedo advertised its coming as soon as the fish was fired, submariners, who depend on stealth for effectiveness and survival, had come to feel that a firing range of about 1,000 to 2,000 yards was the ideal attack distance. They had little use for increased torpedo range and were generally satisfied with the torpedo speed available. Destroyermen, who normally expected to attack maneuverable warships under conditions where both the attacker and the target could see each other, understood that the longer the torpedo took to get to the target, the less was the chance of getting a hit. They would like more range to keep farther from the target, but they were not sure they could hit because the enemy would see the torpedo wake and maneuver out of its path.

The fire control problem for torpedoes is much different from that of gunfire, and much simpler. If the target's course and speed are known, the angle of lead required to produce a hit is easy to calculate—target angle, target speed, and torpedo speed provide the necessary three "knowns" to solve the fire control triangle. There is no requirement to measure range-to-target to produce an accurate torpedo course. Range, of course, is useful in deciding whether a given torpedo can reach the target, in tracking to determine the true course of the target instead of estimating it by observing the angle on the bow, and for calculating the time for the torpedo to reach the target, but accurate range to the target is not necessary to make a good torpedo shot. Thus, if you can see your target, estimate its speed and angle on the bow, you can make a good torpedo shot . . . providing that the target doesn't maneuver and your torpedo can reach it.

As a rule of thumb, destroyers can see each other by eye or masthead radar at about 20,000 yards, cruisers at 25,000 yards, and battleships at 30,000 yards. Torpedoes are excellent weapons against all of them and, with a torpedo of the capability of the Type 93, any ship within sight is in torpedo waters. At long range, a single torpedo has a statistically low probability of hitting, but the same can be said of a single 16-inch projectile or a 1,000-pound bomb, and the comparison of the system cost required for each shot yields interesting figures. The probability of hit is significantly increased when several torpedoes are fired in a spread, each at a certain angle to the right or left of its neighbor, to compensate for errors in estimated target course and speed. An eight-torpedo spread, with 2° between adjacent fish, covers 14° of arc and at 6,000 yards puts a torpedo every 200 yards, the length of a battleship or cruiser, along the track of a crossing target. A 16-fish spread with 1° between torpedoes does the same at 12,000 yards. Several ships firing in a coordinated attack could saturate an enemy formation, even at long range. With large groups of destroyers firing in coordination from several directions, as planned for fleet engagements by all large navies, the crisscrossing of the various torpedo spreads would counter any attempt to comb a single unit's torpedoes.

It was such thinking which caused the Japanese naval staff to adopt the Type 93 as a principal weapon in their fleet and gave them confidence that they could defeat the Americans in a major fleet action. From the mid-1930s they modified their planning, tactics, and training to maximize the use of their secret weapon. Officers and men who were identified as torpedomen were of a special breed. They were carefully selected and progressively trained to become experts.

To fight at night, one had to be able to see in the dark. With their habitual thoroughness, the Japanese studied the problem of night vision and trained their men to maximize their ability to see at low light levels. The human eye is very sensitive, but it has very effective protective devices. It slowly adjusts to the light level it is experiencing, but quickly protects itself should that level increase. A person deep in the woods with no flashlight soon finds he can see quite well from starlight alone. At night a lookout on a darkened ship, away from all sources of artificial light, after an hour on duty finds he can see the small waves on the surface of the sea and, if the intervening air is clear, he can always see the horizon. Striking a match or the momentary use of a flashlight, sets his night vision back dramatically and it takes another twenty minutes or so for his eyes to recover. The "buzz-buzz" before a salvo in a U.S. ship warned everyone to brace for the shock of firing. The "buzz-buzz" in a Japanese ship before the salvo was probably used to order everyone to close his eyes. The Japanese also fired only salvoes at night, never the random cadence of continuous fire.

At night, ships are normally detected by observing their black silhouettes against the lighter sky at the horizon. It is unusual to have enough ambient light to observe more than the silhouette when a ship is at a distance. Moonlight is frequently a disadvantage for detecting the enemy. The eyes of anyone who glances at the moon are temporarily blinded and even the sparkling reflection of moonlight from the dancing waves diminishes night vision.

The color of light one might inadvertently see is also important to night vision. The dark blue lights used pre-war in the U.S. Navy for night lighting about the ship proved to be the worst choice possible, because they blinded in the spectrum of the night light from the sky. Red light was found to be less damaging, but any light at all is a disadvantage.

The most blinding sources of light at night in naval warfare, however, are the flashes from the muzzles of one's own guns and the dazzling electric arcs focused by searchlights. The higher the performance of the propellant powder, the brighter the flash. Various ingredients can cause a great deal of smoke as the propellant burns and help to mask the flash when the gases emerge from the muzzle. This is an advantage at night, and the Japanese developed a flashless powder that was sufficiently effective to preserve much of their night vision and make it difficult for an enemy to see their gun flashes.

There are technical things one can do to increase one's ability to pierce the dark. Binoculars and telescopes in which the rays of light pass through less thickness of glass and are reflected fewer times have fewer losses. Magnification can concentrate what light there is. The Japanese used excellent night glasses as binoculars, had powerful binoculars mounted at lookout stations, and paid particular attention to light losses in the optics of their fire control equipment.

But most of all, the Imperial Japanese Navy was prepared and trained to attack, not defend. The Japanese started their war with the invasion of Manchuria in 1931 and continued working southward. They had hoped to get away with it, but expected to be confronted by the western powers at some time and particularly by the United States, which had been troublesome from the start. The attack on Pearl Harbor was a surgical strike in the middle of a long campaign, intended to paralyze an enemy who was threatening their larger plans. The Greater East Asia Co-Prosperity Sphere was too important to be stopped.

The Imperial Japanese Fleet was designed and organized for a specific series of tasks, which were known in advance. The commander in chief and his principal subordinates were the same in the Solomons campaign as they had been at the time of Pearl Harbor, and this continuity extended down to the commanders of the individual ships. The invasion of New Guinea and the establishment of an outpost in the Solomons to protect the left flank was only a step in the time-sequenced plan that had been developed to take over all of Southeast Asia.

Pilot house instruments of Japanese destroyer Yukikaze *showing the prominent location of two pedestal-mounted, 20-power lookout binoculars at the conning officer's station, indicating the emphasis the Japanese put on optics and night vision. Photo from National Archives.*

Looking north across Iron Bottom Bay, with a U.S. destroyer silhouetted against the shadows of Florida Island, indicating the difficulty of seeing a ship against a land mass in the background. U.S. Naval Institute Photo.

‑⚬ VII ⚬‑
THE TOKYO EXPRESS

Rear Admiral Raizo Tanaka stood on the bridge of his flagship *Naganami* in the late afternoon of 30 November 1942, and studied the rain squall blocking his view of Santa Isabel on his starboard bow. He had been steaming at 30 knots for the last four hours to make his rendezvous off Tassafaronga and he could not afford a delay. But it was getting dark and there was nothing he could do but push ahead as fast as he could. The success of the operation required that his ships deliver their cargo on time. He thought back on his experiences so far.

As commander of Destroyer Squadron Two, he had been in the forefront of the Japanese operations since the beginning. At the time of the attack on Pearl Harbor his squadron had consisted of his flagship, light cruiser *Jintsu,* and Destroyer Divisions Eight, Fifteen, Sixteen, and Eighteen, with a total of 16 destroyers. In January 1942 he had led his squadron to protect the invasion forces during the Menado operations in the Dutch East Indies, then shifted to the invasion of Ambon. His ships had continued their operations to support the capture of Surabaya and to complete the seizure of the Indies. In mid-March they had returned to Japan for overhaul, but were sent to sea briefly after the Doolittle raid.

The entire squadron was next assigned to escort the invasion force for the Midway operation, but after the unbelievable loss of four of the big carriers, the invasion was called off and he had to share the disgrace as he led his ships back to Japan. When the transports and cargo ships were safe, the squadron was sent to the Aleutians to support the capture of Kiska. On the day of the American invasion of Guadalcanal, however, it was ordered back to Yokosuka to prepare for South Seas operations.

In mid-July Vice Admiral Gunichi Mikawa had been put in command of a newly formed Eighth Fleet, to be based at Rabaul and responsible for operations in the Solomon Islands area. As Tanaka approached Truk from the home islands on the 11th of August, with only *Jintsu* and *Kagero* of his squadron, he was ordered to report to Mikawa and become the Commander of the Guadalcanal Reinforcement Force. On the 15th at Truk, while trying to gather his ships and provision them, he received detailed orders from Mikawa to land the Army's renowned Ichiki Detachment at Cape Taivu on Guadalcanal, 18 miles east of Henderson Field. The first 900 of these battle-tested troops were to be transported in six destroyers and landed on the night of the 18th, without artillery or heavy equipment, carrying light packs with only seven days of supplies. The remainder of the detachment, mostly service units with additional supplies, was to be carried in two slow (9-knot) transports escorted by *Jintsu* and two patrol boats.

The Yokosuka Fifth Special Landing Force, with 1,000 additional combat troops, in a fast (13-knot) transport escorted by two patrol boats, would join *Jintsu* en route and the combined force would be unloaded at Taivu on the night of the 23rd. Three destroyers of DesDiv 24 were ordered to join his force on the way south.

The first six destroyers unloaded their troops unopposed on the night of the 18th as scheduled. Three of them headed immediately for Rabaul while the other three stood by to guard the troops ashore. On the morning of the 19th, one of them, *Hagikaze,* was hit by a bomb from a B-17 and damaged so badly Tanaka ordered her to return to Truk under escort of another, *Yamakaze,* leaving only *Kagero* on guard at Taivu. On the 20th *Kagero* was attacked by carrier-based bombers, but although not hit, the attack indicated to the Japanese high command that the Americans were aware of their activity at Taivu.

That same night, Colonel Kiyonao Ichiki led his 900 men in an assault intended to capture Henderson Field. In furious fighting, his troops were repulsed and annihilated. Only some 20 men of a signal unit survived and, after reporting the situation to Rabaul by radio, they fled south across the island through the jungle. Colonel Ichiki burned his regimental colors and committed suicide.

The Commander of the Southeast Area at Rabaul, realizing that an American carrier task force was in the vicinity, ordered Tanaka to reverse course and return to Truk. Almost simultaneously, Eighth Fleet headquarters at Rabaul ordered him to change course to 280° T. He split the difference and came to 320°. Next, *Kagero* reported that 20 American carrier planes had landed at Henderson Field. Tanaka was still scheduled to land his troops on the night of the 23rd and now the enemy had an operational airfield with planes to oppose him.

On the 21st he learned that the Second Fleet, under Vice Admiral Kondo, with its fast main body composed of five heavy cruisers screened by a light cruiser and five destroyers, backed up by a slower group with the battleship *Mutsu,* seaplane carrier *Chitose,* and four destroyers, had been ordered out to meet the Americans. To this was added the Third Fleet Carrier Striking Force, under Vice Admiral Nagumo, with the carriers *Shokaku* and *Zuikaku* plus six destroyers. As these major combatant forces sortied from Truk and turned southeast, Tanaka's landing was postponed until the night of the 24th.

Now somewhat more hopeful of success, Tanaka's small but vital convoy once again reversed course and headed for Guadalcanal. Meanwhile he had replaced *Kagero* off Taivu with *Kawakaze* and *Yunagi.* There was a reconnaissance report of two enemy transports and a light cruiser 160 miles south of Guadalcanal, so Tanaka ordered his two destroyers south to intercept, but they found nothing and returned to duty off Taivu. In the early light of the 22nd, *Kawakaze* torpedoed the U.S. destroyer *Blue* off Lunga Roads—*Blue* had to be scuttled next day.

As Tanaka's force was making its way slowly southward on the 23rd it was sighted and shadowed by American PBYs. He reported the situation, expecting to be ordered to withdraw, but nothing came in from his multiple commanders, so he plodded onward toward his objective throughout the night.

At 0830 on the morning of the 24th, an urgent message was received from Eighth Fleet directing him to turn north to keep out of danger during the carrier battle that was brewing to the east, so again he reversed course. He was subsequently startled to receive, six hours later, instructions from Commander Eleventh Air Fleet, in charge of all land-based air operations in the Solomons, to carry out the landing as ordered that night. Tanaka could only reply that it would be impossible to comply because of the slow speed of his transports, but he again reversed course and headed for Guadalcanal. To complicate matters, atmospheric conditions interfered with radio transmissions, so communication with higher command was delayed.

At 1230 the heavy cruiser *Tone* and the carrier *Ryujo,* escorted by two destroyers, were sighted on the eastern horizon speeding south. *Ryujo*'s planes were to attack Henderson Field in support of the landing and shortly after she passed, she launched her planes. Two hours later, signs of a fierce air battle suddenly appeared to the southeast and in minutes a tall column of smoke announced *Ryujo* had been hit—she sank in the early evening. *Ryujo*'s planes, returning from their attack, circled over Tanaka's force, then flew off to land at Buka, on the northwest tip of Bougainville.

By 1400 news was received that planes from the Third Fleet carriers *Shokaku* and *Zuikaku* were attacking an American force[1] of three carriers, a battleship, seven cruisers, and a number of destroyers near Stewart Island. Returning pilots reported they had set two ships[2] on fire and a surface force was sent from Second Fleet to pursue them. Unable to find the Americans during the night of the 24th, the Second and Third Fleet units turned north and retired toward Truk.

Tanaka's convoy had been ordered to turn to the northeast during the battle, but upon hearing of the damage to the American ships, he swung south again to carry out his basic orders, although he had little expectation that a successful landing could be made.

At 0600 on the 25th, Tanaka's force was still creeping along at 9 knots, 150 miles from Henderson Field. During the night his force had been augmented by the return of *Kagero, Kawakaze,* and *Isokaze* and two smaller ships from DesDiv 30, *Mutsuki* and *Yayoi.* He had hardly transmitted their cruising instructions when six American dive bombers dove out of the clouds at *Jintsu.* Caught unprepared, she was hit heavily forward with near misses amidships. The last bomb hit on the forecastle between guns number one and two, spraying the area with splinters and wreaking havoc on the bridge. Tanaka was knocked unconscious, but when he came to, found himself uninjured. *Jintsu,* although severely damaged, remained on an even keel and her crew quickly got the fire and flooding under control. Her engines were not damaged, but she was unable to fight effectively because of the loss of her forward guns and, with a badly damaged

1   Vice Admiral Fletcher's Task Force Sixty-One, with *Saratoga, Enterprise, Wasp;* battleship *North Carolina*; seven cruisers, and eighteen destroyers.
2   Only *Enterprise* was hit.

bow, could not make high speed. Tanaka ordered *Kagero* alongside and transferred his flag, ordering *Jintsu* to return to Truk.

In the same attack, *Kinryu Maru,* carrying the Yokosuka Fifth Special Landing Force, had been heavily hit, was afire with ammunition exploding, and was near sinking. Tanaka ordered his DesDiv 30 ships plus two patrol boats alongside the stricken transport to take off the troops and crew. As they came alongside, a B-17 appeared and bombed the stationary ships, hitting *Mutsuki,* which sank instantly. *Yayoi* rescued her crew and, along with the patrol boats, took the remaining survivors off *Kinryu Maru* before she too sank. Tanaka ordered all the rescue ships with survivors aboard to head for Rabaul.

Recognizing the futility of landing the remaining auxiliary unit of 300 men on Guadalcanal in view of the annihilation of the Ichiki troops, Tanaka radioed his recommendation to cancel the operation and headed for the Japanese advanced base at Shortland Island at the southeastern tip of Bougainville. Combined and Eighth Fleet commanders concurred with his decision, but he had not even arrived at the anchorage before he received instructions from Eleventh Air Fleet to transport the 300 men to Guadalcanal on the night of the 27th in fast warships.

Though Tanaka thought this was an ill-advised order, he set to work to comply and loaded *Umikaze, Yamakaze,* and *Isokaze* with 390 soldiers and supplies for 1,300. The three destroyers, under the command of Captain Murakami, ComDesDiv 24, had hardly departed Shortland when a message from Eighth Fleet postponed the night of the landing to the 28th. Tanaka replied that the operation was already underway for a landing on the 27th, but Eighth Fleet told him to recall his ships at once, adding that he was sending DesDiv 20 to Shortland to join his command.

Tanaka was so disturbed by the conflicting and contradictory orders he had been receiving that he began to lose faith that a successful operation could be mounted and shared his fears with his friend and former ComDesRon 2, Rear Admiral Goto, ComCruDiv 6, who had arrived at Shortland with his *Aoba* and *Furutaka.* It seemed incredible to both of them that there should not be cooperation between Eighth Fleet and Eleventh Air Fleet, since they were both located at Rabaul, and there seemed to be little coordination between either of them and their superior, Command in Chief Combined Fleet, Admiral Yamamoto, at Truk. Both Tanaka, as commander of the Guadalcanal reinforcement group, and Goto, as commander of the Covering Group, reported to Vice Admiral Mikawa, Commander Outer South Seas Force, who was also Commander Eighth Fleet. Mikawa in turn reported to Vice Admiral Tsukahara, Commander Southeast Area Forces, who was headquartered at Rabaul. Admiral Tsukahara was also Commander Land-Based Air Force and Commander Eleventh Air Fleet. Although the individual flag officer in command was often the same person, the staffs planned, made decisions, and sent messages without conferring with each other. It was maddening.

Successive dispatches finally made it clear why the four DesDiv 20 destroyers had been assigned to his command. At Truk they had loaded the Kawaguchi Detachment from Borneo and were scheduled to land the soldiers at Taivu on the night of the 28th. The troops loaded in Tanaka's ships were to be second wave reinforcements. Tanaka consequently ordered ComDesDiv 24 to take his three ships plus *Isokaze* to be joined by the four ships of DesDiv 20, and make the landing on the 28th. This plan was thwarted when, to save fuel, DesDiv 20 was routed directly from Truk to Guadalcanal. Tanaka consequently had to send Murakami's four ships down the Slot between the two lines of Solomon Islands to Iron Bottom Bay separately.

During the afternoon of the 28th, DesDiv 20, still 80 miles north of Guadalcanal, was attacked by American planes, killing the division commander, sinking *Asagiri,* and damaging *Shirakumo* and *Yugiri.* Their landing was aborted and the surviving ships headed for Shortland. Later in the evening, Captain Murakami, hearing of this, considered it futile to land only the troops embarked in his ships, reversed course, and returned to Shortland. Tanaka was furious at this independent action, which he considered inexcusable, and he reprimanded Murakami severely. He in turn received strongly worded messages of disappointment from his superiors.

The 28th of August brought one welcome change. *Kinugasa,* from CruDiv 6, arrived at Shortland to serve as Tanaka's flagship. Admiral Mikawa had made this change realizing the inadequacy of a destroyer's communication facilities for the growing activities of the reinforcement force. Tanaka shifted his flag from *Kagero* to *Kinugasa* without delay and sent a message of thanks to Mikawa.

Early on the 29th Eighth Fleet ordered, "Use destroyers to transport Army troops." Tanaka immediately ordered Murakami to load his four ships and depart for Taivu at 1000 and land his troops that night. He also ordered two patrol boats to load the remaining 120 troops from the Ichiki Detachment and land them on the night of the 30th.

Meanwhile, Major General Kawaguchi himself, with the main part of his army detachment, arrived in Shortland in the army transport *Sado Maru.* He had been very successful working along the coast of Borneo using large landing barges and he did not think much of moving his troops in destroyers. He insisted on continuing in his army transport to Gizo Harbor in the New Georgia Islands on the south side of the Slot. There he would still be beyond the range of Guadalcanal-based planes and could continue to his objective in barges, using the many islands as cover.

While the midnight conference with General Kawaguchi and his staff was taking place aboard *Kinugasa,* Captain Murakami's four ships plus three ships of DesDiv 11 had successfully landed their troops at Taivu. Two American transports, one cruiser, and two destroyers were reported near Lunga Point, and Admiral Mikawa had sent an order directly to ComDesDiv 24 to attack the enemy force as soon as the landing had been completed. Murakami ignored the order and returned to Shortland. Tanaka summoned him aboard his flagship and demanded an explanation. Murakami said he had not attacked because it was a clear night with a full moon and many American planes had been seen overhead. Tanaka was dumbfounded by his words. He was also overwhelmed with embarrassment, realizing that he would be blamed for his subordinate's lack of courage. He relieved Murakami of his command and had him transferred to the homeland.

On the 30th of August, Tanaka proposed to send the remaining Ikichi troops and an advance force of the Kawaguchi Detachment to Guadalcanal in *Amagiri, Kagero,* and the newly arrived *Yudachi.* General Kawaguchi would not agree to having any of his troops transported in Navy ships, so at 1000, after hours of futile negotiation with the general, Tanaka sailed only *Yudachi,* carrying the Ikichi forces. Mikawa's chief of staff, not knowing of the general's intransigence, bitterly criticized Tanaka in a dispatch.

Overnight an agreement was reached with Commander Seventeenth Army, Kawaguchi's superior, to transport the bulk of the Kawaguchi Detachment in destroyers, the remainder to go in large landing barges. The compromise was transmitted by Eighth Fleet to Tanaka, but, since the message was not addressed to him directly, Kawaguchi still would not agree. Finally on the morning of the 31st, the general gave in, though his regimental commander never did agree, and loading of the troops began. It was noon before the 1,000 troops and their supplies were loaded and the eight destroyers could depart for Guadalcanal.

All troops were landed successfully by midnight and the destroyers returned to Shortland without incident. This was the third time a complete army unit had landed successfully from destroyers.

While his frustrating struggle with the stubborn general was going on, Tanaka received a message from Combined Fleet in Truk ordering ComDes-Ron 3 to proceed from Rabaul and upon arrival, ComDesRon 2 was to relinquish his command and proceed to Truk in *Yugiri*. On the 31st of August, Rear Admiral Hashimoto arrived with light cruiser *Sendai* with DesDiv 18 of his squadron and, after a brief but correct ceremony, relieved him. Tanaka immediately departed for Truk in *Yugiri,* accompanied by his staff.

He made the voyage to Truk with heavy heart, feeling he was being relieved for his many losses and repeated failures to land reinforcements when desired, but tried to be philosophical, recognizing that he was totally exhausted and needed time to recuperate. He was pleasantly surprised upon arrival, however, to find that replacement ships were being assembled to bring DesRon 2 up to its original strength and that he was being assigned to command the direct escort for CruDivs 4, 5, and 8 in the Second Fleet. The light cruiser *Isuzu* was to be his flagship and the newly organized DesDiv 11, composed of the big "super" destroyers *Takanami, Makinami,* and *Naganami,* had been added to his command.

In the Solomons, the Kawaguchi Detachment was finally assembled on Guadalcanal and a general attack to recapture Henderson Field was launched on the 12th of September. The fighting was vicious and the attack almost succeeded, but in the end it was thrown back, with the famous detachment decimated. At sea, the main opposing forces didn't engage, but Japanese submarine *I-19* torpedoed *Wasp* on the 15th and, after being swept by unbelievable fires, the charred hulk was sunk by the Americans at the end of the day. On the 23rd, the Japanese main forces returned to Truk to replenish.

By now the Japanese army had come to realize that Guadalcanal could not be recaptured by small units, so Lieutenant General Maruyama's 2nd Division was brought from Java to Shortland. These troops were to be transported to their objective in six high-speed transports escorted by the reinforcement force. The landing was to take place on the night of the 14th of October with a general assault on the Americans planned for the 22nd.

Both Second and Third Fleets sortied from Truk on 11 October and Cru-Div 6, with *Aoba, Kinugasa,* and *Furutaka* and two destroyers were sent ahead with orders to bombard the airfield that same night. They were met by Admiral Scott's force to the northwest of Savo Island, as described previously, where a fierce battle was fought and the bombardment group turned back. The Japanese lost the heavy cruiser *Furutaka* and the destroyer *Shirakumo* sank, with the flagship *Aoba* badly damaged and Rear Admiral Goto killed, believing they had sunk one American cruiser, damaged one, and sunk a destroyer. The next day the destroyer *Murakumo* was heavily damaged as the force made its way toward Shortland, and when the destroyer *Natsugumo* came back to help her, she in turn was bombed and sunk.

Although the losses were serious, the neutralizing of the airfield was essential if successful reinforcement of the troops already ashore was to be achieved, so on the night of the 13th of October, the 14-inch battleships *Kongo* and *Haruna,* equipped with a newly developed bombardment projectile that produced firecracker-like shrapnel when bursting, were sent to do the job. Tanaka, in *Isuzu,* with seven other ships of DesRon 2, accompanied the battleships as they sailed from Truk. The big ships squared away at 16,000 meters and treated Henderson Field to an hour and a half of devastating bombardment. The entire jungle burst into flames as planes, fuel, and ammunition exploded together in an all-consuming conflagration. Frantic plain-language radio transmissions were overheard reporting tremendous damage. Upon completion of their rounds, the bombardment force withdrew, passing to the east of Savo. Some motor torpedo boats came out from Tulagi, but the destroyer *Naganami* drove them away.

On the night of the 14th, cruisers *Chokai* and *Kinugasa* repeated the treatment and the six fast transports carrying the 2nd Division arrived and started unloading at Tassafaronga. They were attacked at dawn by carrier planes coming from the south—three of them escaped to return to Shortland, but three of them had to be run aground, where they were bombed and set afire.

On the night of the 15th, *Myoko* and *Maya* of CruDiv 6, again with Tanaka and DesRon 2 escorting, poured 800 more 8-inch shells into the battered airfield, but the results were much less spectacular than the big bombardment by the battleships. There were moves and countermoves on the 16th and the fleet withdrew to the equator for refueling. It returned to positions both to the northeast and the northwest of Guadalcanal for the general attack on the 22nd, but, because the troops were having more trouble getting through the jungle than had been anticipated, the push was delayed until the 24th. The attack jumped off as scheduled and, because of early, though erroneous, reports of its success, DesRon 4 charged down the Slot from the northwest to support the troops ashore. The army's assault was repulsed with heavy losses and at dawn DesRon 4 was caught before it could get out of range. In the attack by American bombers, light cruiser *Yura* was so heavily damaged she had to be sunk.

At dawn on the 26th of October, Second and Third Fleet air reconnaissance found the American Carrier Task Force 200 miles north of the Santa Cruz Islands to the east of the Solomons. The force was reported to be composed of three carriers, two battleships, five cruisers, and twelve destroyers. Without delay two attack groups were launched, which hit both *Hornet* and *Enterprise,* the first so heavily that she burned most of the day. The returning pilots also reported setting the third carrier afire, sinking a battleship, two cruisers, and a destroyer as well as shooting down a number of planes.

The American planes in turn had scored hits on both *Shokaku* and *Zuiho,* setting them afire and rendering their flight decks useless, and the cruiser *Chikuma* was damaged so badly she had to retire. The Second Fleet was sent forward to finish the job, but found only the smoldering wreck of *Hornet,* which was eventually sunk by destroyers *Makigumo* and *Akigumo* the next morning. Tanaka led his DesRon 2 in a high-speed chase to the south hoping to catch the enemy formation in the night, but he found nothing and had to rejoin the rest of the fleet. Search operations were continued throughout the 27th, but no trace of the American force was found and all ships returned to Truk.

The Japanese losses by the end of October, both ashore and at sea, necessitated refreshment and reorganization. Both DesRons 3 and 4 had suffered heavy losses, and those ships which remained were in no condition to continue. As a consequence, as soon as his ships were replenished, Tanaka sailed from Truk in his flagship *Isuzu* with *Oyashio, Kuroshio,* and *Kagero* of DesDiv 15; *Kawakaze* and *Suzukaze* of DesDiv 24; and *Takanami, Makinami,* and *Naganami* of DesDiv 31 to replace the two battered squadrons. Upon arrival at Shortland he called on Vice Admiral Mikawa, who had just arrived in *Chokai,* and was informed that he would once again command the entire reinforcement force.

The Seventeenth Army had worked out a plan for reinforcing the troops remaining on Guadalcanal with the fresh 38th Division, and as soon as everything was in place, to mount a frontal attack on the Americans. After several changes in plans, it was decided to send an advance unit of 1,300 men to Tassafaronga in 11 destroyers on the night of the 7th of November. Though Tanaka had planned to lead the force himself, he was ordered to remain at Shortland, so the force was commanded by ComDesDiv 15, Captain Torajiro Sato. The ships left Shortland with orders to pass north of Choiseul and Santa Isabel before heading south for Guadalcanal, but were heavily attacked by carrier-based bombers in the afternoon. Due to the fierce defense by their six escorting fighters, all of which were shot down during the melee, all ships managed to escape damage and the troops were put ashore at Tassafaronga without loss during the night.

On the 10th, Lieutenant General Sano, commander of the 38th Division, and 600 of his troops were transported in *Makinami* and *Suzukaze* and, although heavily attacked with both bombs and aerial torpedoes en route and by four MTBs[3] at their destination, were safely landed at Tassafaronga at night.

Although reconnaissance had reported an American carrier force to the south, when the main body of the 38th Division, embarked in eleven army transports, arrived in Shortland on the evening of the 12th, Tanaka, flying his flag in *Hayashio,* ordered them immediately to set course for Guadalcanal, protecting them with all the destroyers he had.

To neutralize Henderson Field for this crucial landing, Admiral Abe led his battleships *Hiei* and *Kirishima* with DesRons 4 and 10 to Iron Bottom Bay to repeat the performance of the big bombardment a month before. They were just coming to their firing course when an enemy force of cruisers and destroyers (Callaghan's column) thrust its way into their midst. Flagship *Hiei* had gotten off only two salvoes at the enemy when she was heavily struck by shells from an enemy cruiser, which knocked out her steering gear and made her fire control system inoperative. She spent the rest of the night cruising in circles, out of control. Destroyers *Akatsuki* and *Yudachi* were sunk, and *Amatsukaze* and *Ikazuchi* were severely damaged. With such heavy losses, the bombardment was abandoned and Abe, shifting to a destroyer, started to withdraw his force. Two enemy cruisers and several destroyers were thought to have been sunk. Soon after dawn on the 13th, American planes started raining bombs down on the crippled *Hiei* and continued all day until it became clear that she could not be extricated. Her crew was taken off by attending destroyers and the proud old battleship was scuttled.

When it was realized that the planned bombardment had been thwarted, Combined Fleet postponed the landing until the night of the 14th and directed Tanaka to turn his force around and return to Shortland. He got back about

---

3   Motor Torpedo Boats

noon on the 13th and an hour later started herding his eleven loaded transports back toward Guadalcanal again. That night heavy cruisers *Maya* and *Suzuya* shot everything they had at Henderson Field, but Tanaka had a premonition that fate was not on his side. He had arranged his transports in four parallel columns and they were steaming steadily at eleven knots, with his destroyers deployed ahead and to both sides for protection. At dawn a combat air patrol of Zeroes appeared overhead.

The day started with an attack by two B-17s and four carrier-based bombers, three of which were shot down by the Zeroes, but no bombs hit his ships. An hour later two more dive-bombers came in, but both were shot down. Shortly afterward a large group of enemy planes was sighted to the southwest, so Tanaka ordered his destroyers to make smoke and instructed the transport columns to take evasive action. But these planes were going for the Eighth Fleet covering force, which was about 50 miles to the west—*Kinugasa* was sunk, *Isuzu* heavily damaged, and *Chokai* and *Maya* lightly damaged. Following the attack, the covering force retired to Shortland, leaving Tanaka to continue down the Slot alone.

Later in the morning his convoy was attacked by a total of 41 planes—eight B-17s, eight torpedo planes, and the rest dive-bombers and fighters. Transports *Canberra Maru* and *Nagara Maru* were torpedoed and sank. *Sado Maru,* carrying the army commander, was crippled by bombs. After the survivors of the two sunken transports were picked up, *Sado Maru* turned back toward Shortland, escorted by destroyers *Amagiri* and *Mochizuki.*

Two hours later the attackers returned, this time with eight B-17s and two dozen dive-bombers. *Brisbane Maru* was set afire and soon sank. Within an hour six more B-17s and five carrier bombers appeared and sank *Shinanogawa Maru* and *Arizona Maru.* Other smaller attacks came in with no added damage, but a half hour before sunset 21 planes came in, including four B-17s. *Nako Maru* was set afire and soon went down.

As night settled in and the air attacks were finished for the day, Tanaka took stock. His force had been attacked by more than 100 enemy planes, six of his eleven transports were sunk and one sent back, some 400 of his men had been killed, but amazingly over 5,000 of the crews and embarked troops had been rescued by his destroyers. His ships were scattered and their crews exhausted. But he was too deep into enemy waters to be able to withdraw without further losses and any reinforcement was vital to the Japanese fighters on Guadalcanal. In addition, reconnaissance reported four enemy cruisers and four destroyers steaming northward at high speed to the east of Guadalcanal. As he pondered his precarious situation, any doubt he might have had was resolved by a direct order from Combined Fleet: "Continue toward Guadalcanal." He assembled his four remaining transports and, with only *Hayashio* and the three ships of DesDiv 15, he pushed on toward his objective.

Although the outcome of his operation appeared hopeless, his spirits were lifted when he learned that the Second Fleet was coming south at full speed to intercept the enemy force. This meant that the flagship *Atago,* battleship *Kirishima,* two heavies from CruDiv 4, and several destroyers would be directly supporting his landing. About midnight, with visibility of about seven kilometers, he sighted his guardians taking station ahead as they approached Savo Island.

As the advance unit of destroyers entered Iron Bottom Bay passing to the east of Savo, it contacted several enemy heavy cruisers. Heavy gunfire was exchanged and the sky lighted up with flares. The rest of the Second Fleet ships, coming down to the west of Savo, soon joined in the action and *Atago*'s searchlight quickly revealed that they were engaging not cruisers, but *North Carolina*–class battleships.

Seeing the battle evolve on the horizon ahead, Tanaka reversed course for his transports to keep them out of harm's way, but sent Captain Sato with the three ships of DesDiv 15 to join the fray. Moments later, he received radio instructions from Combined Fleet to withdraw his transports as he was already doing.

The battle lasted about an hour, but as soon as the firefight moved west out of his path, Tanaka, in his one remaining destroyer, *Hayashio,* led his four surviving transports at full speed toward Tassafaronga.

The original plan had been for the transports to arrive so unloading could begin about midnight and be completed in two hours. From his present position, it would be impossible to arrive at the planned debarkation point and begin unloading before dawn. He knew daylight would bring swarms of American bombers from Henderson Field—it was only a few miles from Tassafaronga. The only way to land the troops quickly and prevent the valuable cargoes from joining the ships at the bottom of Iron Bottom Bay was to run his ships aground. The concept of running aground four of Japan's best transports was, to say the least, unprecedented, but Tanaka could think of no other solution. He radioed his recommendation to his superiors and hoped they would reply in time. He could see Savo Island ahead and Guadalcanal was only a few miles beyond. Eighth Fleet, with Commander Seventeenth Army at his elbow, replied with a flat "No," but Second Fleet, in direct charge of this operation, replied, "Run aground and unload troops."

Arriving at first light, he deployed his transports in a line abreast and ran them aground almost simultaneously on the stretches of beach from below Tassafaronga up halfway to Doma Cove. He then assembled his destroyers, which had returned after the battle, and headed north, passing east of Savo.

As expected, the American bombers soon arrived and the grounded transports were set afire, but all the troops, with their light arms and ammunition, and a part of the needed provisions, were landed successfully. As his destroyers sped back to Shortland, their captains signaled their reports of the battle with the American battleships. It appeared that two enemy battleships had been damaged by torpedoes from DesDiv 11 and *Oyashio* of DesDiv 15. In addition, in the earlier stages of the battle, two heavy cruisers and one destroyer had been sunk, with one heavy cruiser and one destroyer seriously damaged. Even though the Japanese had lost the battleship *Kirishima* and the destroyer *Ayanami,* the returning warriors thought this third battle of the Solomons had ended in their favor.

With more than 10,000 men ashore on Guadalcanal and no success in supplying them by conventional transport, the Japanese high command was ready to try anything. Urgent requests for every type of material and medical supply arrived daily and by the end of November food was so scarce that the troops were reduced to eating wild plants and animals. Everyone was on the verge of starvation, sick lists increased, and even the healthy were exhausted. Supply by air could not be undertaken because of American air superiority. Supply by submarine, although used with some success, could not approach the volume needed. It was consequently decided to try to supply the troops by destroyer, using the drum method.

There were plenty of large metal drums or other containers with removable tops in the forward area, so these were sterilized, filled with basic foodstuffs or medical supplies, but leaving enough air to ensure buoyancy, and loaded on the decks of the destroyers. They were then linked together with strong rope to form a long chain that could be pushed over the side. Once in the water, the chain of drums could be pulled ashore by the troops on the beach, after the end of the rope had been passed to them by ship's boat. The idea was tested and found to be practical, so it was decided to use the drum method at Guadalcanal. Tanaka was ordered to make the first run on the night of the 30th of November.

Of the eight destroyers available for the supply run, six were loaded with 200 to 240 drums each and had to unload all of their reserve torpedoes to compensate, thus cutting their available punch in half, but *Takanami,* selected to be the advance picket ship, and *Naganami,* Tanaka's flagship for this operation, carried no cargo and thus were fully ready for battle.

Tanaka had sailed from Shortland before dawn and headed east at a leisurely pace, passing north of the Solomons, in an effort to hide his intentions. As expected, he was found and shadowed by American long-range reconnaissance planes, but he hoped his ruse had worked. Around noon, unable to hold off any longer, he shaped course southward and increased speed to 24 knots, the best high-cruising speed of his older ships. It began to rain and he hoped the clouds concealed his new course. At 1500 he upped his speed to 30 knots for the final run to Guadalcanal. He was scheduled to be off Tassafaronga and Segilau (Doma Cove) at exactly 2330 and the desperate men ashore would be waiting.

During the afternoon, reconnaissance reported twelve enemy destroyers and nine transports in the Guadalcanal-Tulagi area so he alerted his ships and instructed them, "There is a great possibility of an encounter with the enemy tonight. In such an event, utmost efforts will be made to destroy the enemy without regard for unloading supplies."

There were no more messages from his superiors. Eighth Fleet and Eleventh Air Fleet were silent. Even Combined Fleet had sent no messages. This time he was on his own. No cruisers or battleships to restrict his motions, no lumbering transports to slow him down. Just destroyers and destroyermen—the best in the Imperial Fleet. Captain Sato, ComDesDiv 15, who had proved himself many times in the last months, was flying his broad command pennant in *Makinami* and would lead the Tassafaronga group. He had selected Captain Toshio Shimizu, ComDesDiv 31, in *Takanami,* commanded by the outstanding Commander Masami Ogura, to stand guard as picket ship to cover the operation. Captain Giichiro Nakahara, ComDesDiv 24, would command the Segilau group. In his flagship *Naganami,* with battle-tested Commander Shimamoto in command, he would be free to move as he saw fit with full confidence in his subordinate commanders.

He looked back at his long column of ships and admired their power and beauty. *Naganami, Takanami,* and *Makinami* were of the *Yugumo* class, among the latest and biggest destroyers in the Imperial Fleet. Long, sleek, and displacing 2,077 tons, they had 52,000 HP and their speed was listed as 35–45 knots. Their main battery was two center line quadruple torpedo mounts and they had six 5-inch dual-purpose guns mounted in three twin mounts, one forward and two, superposed, aft, plus four 25-mm AA guns in twin mounts. In profile they rose in steps from a high forecastle, over the forward 5-inch, over the forward 25-mm platform, up a double step to the top of the bridge structure, atop of which was a high dual-purpose gun director. Abaft the mast they swept aft in a long low structure containing the torpedo mounts and re-load arrangements, finally dropping over the after two 5-inch mounts to the fantail and a rounded cruiser stern. Their very substantial tripod mast legs straddled the after portion of the bridge structure, which was followed by a large forward stack reaching to the level of the director platform, and then, with a relatively long gap, a second, smaller stack. The mainmast, just forward on 5-inch mount number two, was hardly more than a flagstaff, rising only to the height of the forward stack. They really looked like small cruisers.

Kagero, Kuroshio, and *Oyashio* were of the *Kagero* class. These ships, which had been ordered in 1937 and 1938, two years earlier than the *Yugumo*s, were only slightly lighter and had the same engines and armament as the newer class. They had a slightly different appearance, however, because the bridge structure was shorter fore and aft, leaving the tripod mast standing completely clear, and the forward stack was fatter and slightly lower.

Kawakaze and *Suzukaze* were of the 1934 building program, and displacing 1,580 tons, were powered with only 42,000 HP, giving them a top speed of 34 knots. They had one less 5-inch gun, number two mount being a single, and both after mounts were on the main deck, not superposed.

His plan for the landing operation was quite simple. He was sending *Takanami* 10 miles ahead to scout the area and stand guard while the other ships unloaded. *Naganami* would lead *Kawakaze* and *Suzukaze* to their drop-off point just seaward of Doma Reef because she was better equipped to navigate close inshore, then she would be free to back up *Takanami*. Captain Sato would take *Makinami, Kagero, Oyashio,* and *Kuroshio* to their discharge point off Tassafaronga. Tanaka planned to hold his column formation with the flagship at the head until *Takanami* reported the sound to be clear of the enemy, then disperse to the discharge points. At 2300, with *Takanami* ahead and already probing the sound, he ordered his ships to break formation and proceed as assigned. *Naganami* sheered right and slowed to lead the way for the two smaller ships. *Takanami* had already slowed and was steady on her course to the southeast, every eye and instrument straining to find something against the eastern horizon. Captain Sato continued forward toward Tassafaronga with his four ships, holding his speed at 30 knots.

Rear Admiral Raizo Tanaka, IJN, commander of the Japanese forces at the Battle of Tassafaronga. Photo from the Naval Historical Center.

HAMANAMI off Maizuru. 10.10.43. Note Type 22 radar on top of fore tripod and 25 mm. A.A. in front of bridge. [I.W.M.

Yugumo class

Ordered in 1939 and 1941, the design of this class was that of the KAGERO class with added refinements. The elevation of the main guns was increased from 55 degrees to 75 degrees and the bridge was streamlined, reducing wind resistance and improving stability. The tripod mast was also modified to carry radar. During the war all ships in this class were fitted with a Type No. 13 radar, a Type No. 22 radar and degaussing cables.

In 1943 the number of light A.A. was increased to 6—25 mm. In 1943-44 the "X" turret was removed and replaced by triple 25 mm. A.A., the light A.A. being increased to 15—25 mm. A.A. After June 1944 the spare torpedoes were removed from all ships. Some vessels were modified to carry between 15 and 28—25 mm. A.A. and 4—13 mm. guns, whilst in others "Y" turret and the A.A. occupying the "X" turret position were removed and replaced by 2 twin 4·7 in. D.P. guns, 12—25 mm. A.A. being carried.

The 8 named units ordered in the 1941 Programme were cancelled before they were laid down and a further 8 units of a slightly modified type ordered as Nos. 5041-5048 under the 1942 Modified Programme also suffered the same fate.

Displacement: 2,077 tons.
Dimensions: 366 (pp) 391 (oa) × 35 × 12 ft.
Machinery: 2-shaft geared Turbines, S.H.P. 52,000 = 35½ knots.
Armament: 6—5 in. D.P. (3 × 2), 4—25 mm. A.A. (2 × 2) guns; 8—24 in. T.T. (2 × 4); 4 depth charge throwers and 36 depth charges.
Complement: 228.

Japanese Yugumo-class Destroyer. Makinami, Naganami, *and* Takanami *were destroyers of this class. Photos and data from Japanese Warships of World War II, by A. J. Watts.*

Japanese Kagero-class destroyer. Kagero, Kuroshio, *and* Oyashio *were destroyers of this class.*
Photo from The National Institute for Defense Studies, Tokyo, Japan.

Japanese Umikaze-class destroyer. Kawakaze *and* Suzukaze *were destroyers of this class.*
Photo from The National Institute for Defense Studies, Tokyo, Japan.

VIII

THE OTHER SIDE

As soon as *Kawakaze* and *Suzukaze* found their markers off Doma and slowed to lower their boats, Tanaka instructed *Naganami* to move out toward *Takanami* to have some sea room if anything happened. They could see the red and green running lights of three aircraft circling low over the water near Tulagi, so the Americans must be up to something. *Naganami* cut under the stern of the last of Sato's ships as they continued ahead.

At 2312 *Takanami* broke the tense radio silence with, "Sighted what appear to be enemy ships, bearing 100 degrees." She was still 5,000 yards ahead and a bit further off shore, but she was clearly visible. Tanaka stared into the night. The horizon was somewhat lighter in that sector, between the huge shadow of Guadalcanal on the right and the lumps to the left that marked Florida Island and its lesser offshoots, but he could see nothing. The radio crackled again: "Seven enemy destroyers sighted."

Without a moment's delay Tanaka transmitted to all ships, "Stop unloading. Take battle stations." His column had already broken up. The two smaller ships were stopped off of Doma and Sato's four ships were passing *Takanami*, with crews already in the boats and half the men on deck preparing to handle the drums. He could imagine the turmoil. But these men had been through months of combat—he was sure there'd be no delay when the call to battle stations was sounded.

The minutes ticked on—every eye straining to find a shadow. "Ship sighted. Sharp on the port bow." *Naganami*'s lookouts had the enemy. Tanaka raised his glasses. He could easily distinguish several individual ships against the lighter portion of the sky. He gauged the ships against the field of his binoculars—if they were destroyers, he estimated the range at about eight kilometers.

Suddenly there were brilliant gun flashes from the left-hand ship of the enemy force. In a moment the next ship to the right joined in. Bright flares began to fill the sky between *Takanami* and the enemy, blinding the eye until all that could be seen were the flashes of gunfire. Huge geysers of spray arose near *Takanami* and she opened fire in return. Tanaka radioed the general signal, "Close and attack."

As *Naganami* surged forward to the command for full speed, Tanaka could see more flashes on the enemy ships. *Takanami*'s shells were hitting. A tornado of shells began to fall about his flagship and she opened fire. He could see the flash of hits on the second and third ships of the enemy column. The crash of *Naganami*'s own gunfire shook the ship almost as roughly as the enemy shells bursting close aboard. The heavy smoke from the forward guns blanked his view for several seconds after each salvo, but at least he wasn't blinded by his own weapons.

Takanami was drawing the concentrated fire from several ships and the water around her was a cauldron of erupting explosions. She was hit and flames leaped skyward, but her guns kept lashing at the enemy. Sato's ships, ahead to starboard, were getting their share too. It was unbelievable that his flagship could survive the rain of shells falling around her, but she hadn't yet been touched.

Naganami's searchlight flashed on for a moment and caught an enemy ship in its beam—a cruiser on the opposite course. Captain Shimamoto ordered, "Right full rudder," to bring her around to parallel. As she heeled deeply into the turn, now moving at over 30 knots, an increased blizzard of shells fell about her, but still none hit. It was almost like daylight with numerous flares in the sky—the smoke trails as they fell formed the strands of a curtain between the adversaries.

Takanami was now burning steadily with frequent large explosions ripping her apart. Most of her bridge structure was riddled and in flames—Tanaka knew the casualties must be terrible. She had pivoted to starboard and was almost dead in the water, but her smoke generator at her stern kept spewing out clouds of dense smoke, adding to the growing pall.

As *Naganami* completed her turn the starboard lookout shouted, "Torpedo wake to starboard." Tanaka's eyes swept the shimmering water—one deadly wake just ahead, a second which must have passed under the ship, and more to the right—but no explosion. In fact, the hail of fire moved away as his flagship steadied on a northwesterly course and the flames and smoke from *Takanami* blanked the flashes of enemy guns.

A bright white tower of flame leapt skyward from the leading enemy destroyer. It lighted the entire sound. He could see the other ships as in daylight—two destroyers, a cruiser, another destroyer, another cruiser, and two smaller destroyers. He pointed toward the first cruiser in the din of gunfire and exploding shells, but Shimamoto needed no instructions, he was already coming right to attack.

A second huge column of flame leapt upward beside the first, revealing another destroyer had been hit. *Takanami* must have gotten her torpedoes off before she was crippled. But a new hurricane of incoming shells landed just astern in *Naganami's* wake. She must have been doing at least 40 knots. Then the first cruiser passed in front of the blazing enemy ships. It wasn't a cruiser, it was a *Texas*-class battleship. Her entire length was silhouetted against the flames—two massive turrets forward, imposing bridge structure, unmistakable tripod mast topped by a heavy crow's nest, two prominent stacks, lesser mainmast, and two more turrets aft. Shimamoto shouted his orders to his torpedo officer: "Get the big one."

Naganami bore in until the range had reduced to four kilometers, then she came left and launched a full salvo of eight torpedoes—they couldn't miss at this range. Shimamoto continued his turn to put his target astern and called the engine room to give him everything they had. Tanaka was sure she was making her full 45 knots as she headed just to the right of Cape Esperance. Shells fell about her to both sides, but mostly astern. It was unbelievable that of the hundreds of projectiles that had hit close aboard, none had hit. The ship had been severely shaken by near misses, but the only actual damage was a few shrapnel holes in one of her stacks.

By the time the firing started, Captain Sato, in *Makinami,* was 2,000 yards past *Takanami,* and about to cut his speed to approach Tassafaronga. Instead, he held his 30 knots and as soon as the gun flashes outlined the enemy column, he came left to put the enemy on his beam. Shells began to fall near *Kuroshio,* last of his four ships, but after a couple of minutes, they stopped. As the canopy of star shells off his port quarter illuminated the scene, he could see *Takanami* had been badly hit and was burning. A row of tall geysers rose off his quarter as a salvo of large-caliber shells smashed into the water a few hundred meters short. Fifteen seconds later, sharp cracks shattered the air as a salvo passed close overhead and erupted to starboard. Two more salvoes produced walls of water between *Kuroshio* and *Oyashio* next astern, but neither ship was hit.

One after the other, twin columns of fire rose from the head of the enemy column, then the battleship appeared. The range was obviously long, but the older American battleships could only make 21 knots and she was plainly on the opposite course, so *Kuroshio* took a chance and fired two Long Lance torpedoes, hoping for luck. Sato wanted to be closer, so he split his division into two attack sections and, with only *Makinami* and *Kagero*, came around to the right to stalk his enemy and plan his attack.

Oyashio's captain already had his plan, so he led *Kuroshio* around in a sharp course reversal and cranked on 35 knots. The enemy battleship was obviously the best target and after revealing itself clearly in silhouette against the flames of the two lead destroyers, it kept its position updated by the huge flashes of regular salvoes. Eleven minutes after *Kuroshio*'s two shots and now finally past the flames and smoke of *Takanami*, *Oyashio* fired a carefully aimed salvo of eight torpedoes at the battleship. Her whole crew felt confident her torpedoes would find their mark as the two ships continued westward to pass close aboard Cape Esperance.

Off Doma, Tanaka's order to stop unloading caught *Kawakaze* and *Suzukaze* with their boats in the water and gun crews on deck standing by the cargo drums. It would take more time to recover the boats than to get the drums into the water, so both captains ordered the drums pushed over. As the boats cleared the water, the first enemy shells started landing. Both captains ordered, "Emergency speed ahead." The salvoes landing near them were from large-caliber guns and *Takanami* was exploding just two miles ahead. *Suzukaze* sighted several ships well to the left of the main enemy column and commenced firing her 5-inch battery at them. *Kawakaze* led the pair in a sharp course reversal to the left.

As they settled on their course toward Cape Esperance they could plainly see the column of enemy ships deep on their starboard quarter by the intermittent flashes of their guns, but the guns on their beam were no longer firing and they could see nothing in the glare of the falling flares. When the huge fires erupted on the two lead ships, they had a steady point of aim, then the battleship revealed itself in silhouette. It was obviously on a parallel course and its speed couldn't be more than about 20 knots. What luck.

USS Salt Lake City *(CA-25), USS* Pensacola *(CA-24), and USS* New Orleans *(CA-32), nested together at Pearl Harbor in 1943, showing how much taller* Pensacola *was than the New Orleans–class ship and how much larger her mast top structures were. This certainly contributed to the Japanese identification of* Pensacola *as a battleship while* Minneapolis *and* New Orleans *were identified as large destroyers. Photo from National Archives.*

USS Pensacola *(CA-24), top photo. USS* Texas *(BB-35), bottom photo. At night they could be confused. Photos from National Archives.*

Bubbling torpedo wakes slashed along the shimmering reflection of the flames, heading directly for *Suzukaze*. She sheered hard left, risking the reefs to port, while the crew awaited the fated explosion. The wakes extended shoreward and soon there were two big explosions in the water near the reef, but she had not been hit so she came back to the right to follow her leader.

The old American battleship offered an excellent target for *Kawakaze*'s torpedomen. After tracking her carefully through half a dozen main battery salvoes and double-checking all settings on the torpedo director, they fired a full salvo of eight fish at her. The big ship seemed to be firing at a target to the left, but she held her course and successive sights showed no change in speed. A bit more than five minutes after the first fish hit the water, *Kawakaze*'s crew shouted with joy as flames leapt 500 meters up the mainmast of their quarry and then the whole aft end of the ship burst into flame.

Oyashio and *Kuroshio* five miles astern, watched the explosions with satisfaction; it was just the time for *Oyashio*'s torpedoes to hit. As the flames grew it was clear that the target had received a mortal blow, so they searched for other quarry. Beyond the battleship which had been hit, a cruiser, or perhaps another battleship had been firing. *Kuroshio* had been tracking her as she fired and now she could be seen against the horizon just to the right of Savo Island. She took aim at the shadow and fired her last four torpedoes.

When Captain Sato saw the explosion on the battleship, he turned *Makinami* and *Kagero* toward the conflagration to finish her off, passing west of the still blazing *Takanami*. As the range closed, he could see that the big ship was listing heavily to port, had turned left, and was now heading almost directly toward him. But *Makinami*'s crew could not get the cargo drums clear of the torpedo mounts and the range was dropping drastically. He decided to hold *Makinami* off at a safer distance while the crew worked to clear the torpedoes. *Oyashio* and *Kuroshio* were about two miles ahead and closer inshore, so at 2345 *Makinami* came left paralleling them and let *Kagero* dash in alone for the kill.

Two minutes later, night turned to daylight as the greatest explosion of this tumultuous night blasted skyward several kilometers beyond the burning battleship, just to the right of Savo. *Kagero* continued her charge as the flames identified another battleship. She bored in, fired four torpedoes at close range, and finished the job by adding a few salvoes from her guns.

As *Naganami* raced westward clearing the battle area, she was chased by regular nine-gun salvoes from one of the enemy heavy ships. They would have hit in range, but they were off in deflection. It was in violation of everything Tanaka had learned about major caliber gunnery—the Emperor must have interceded with the gods!

As *Kawakaze* and *Suzukaze* came abreast Cape Esperance they received the same treatment, and a few moments later, several bubbling torpedo wakes were sighted close aboard. But miraculously, only *Takanami* of all eight of Tanaka's ships received any significant damage. It was incredible, considering the intensity of the American fire and the duration of the gun battle.

At the pre-arranged rendezvous, Tanaka gathered his ships, but repeated calls elicited no response from *Takanami*. Fearing the worst, he sent *Oyashio* and *Kuroshio* back to assist and save her crew. About 0115 they found *Takanami* still smoldering, but afloat, and put boats in the water to rescue survivors. *Kuroshio* was about to go alongside when an enemy group of two cruisers and three destroyers appeared at such close range that neither side dared fire. The two Japanese destroyers, with no torpedoes remaining, were forced to withdraw, leaving many *Takanami* survivors, who made their way in cutters and rafts to friendly shore positions on Guadalcanal.

A shattered *Takanami* finally slipped to her watery grave an hour after her would-be saviors had left the sound. Tanaka's remaining seven ships returned to Shortland at 0830 and confirmed by daylight that they had not been damaged except for the few unimportant holes in *Naganami*'s after stack. The Admiral radioed to his superiors the tragic loss of a gallant destroyer, but estimated the American losses as one battleship, one cruiser, and one destroyer sunk, with one cruiser and three destroyers heavily damaged.

Although the Japanese felt they had fought well against the enemy force, which they believed consisted of a battleship in the center with several cruisers and destroyers deployed both fore and aft, the supply mission was thwarted. The drum system of re-supply was used on several occasions after this battle, but the percentage of drums actually being hauled ashore was very disappointing. In the end, it was realized that the troops ashore could not be supplied unless the Japanese could control both the sea around Guadalcanal and the air above it. A month after this fateful battle, the high command decided to admit defeat and withdraw.

─ IX ─
THE TORPEDO
PROBLEM

I f the American torpedoes had been used wisely and well, any naval officer would know that the outcome of this battle would have been different. Had Commander Cole led his destroyers in to closer range to allow the high-speed setting, had Admiral Wright released him to fire when he first requested permission, had Admiral Wright held his cruisers back to give the destroyers a chance to complete their attack or delayed opening fire long enough to let the torpedoes do their work, it would have made not one iota of difference.

The ten torpedoes fired by *Fletcher,* the eight by *Perkins,* and the six eventually fired by *Drayton,* although carefully groomed by skilled torpedo gangs and fired with perfect precision, could not have damaged the enemy because they were fatally flawed. Their exploders were unreliable and the fish ran too deep by at least 10 feet. The dedicated men in those four lead destroyers were sent in harm's way with weapons that wouldn't work. They had been sent into battle with wet powder.

The saga of the development and testing of the torpedoes of the U.S. Navy in the years before World War II is an unbelievable concatenation of ambitious dreams, intellectual courage, bright ideas, limited knowledge, faulty design, inadequate testing, uncritical faith, unquestioning loyalty, intellectual arrogance, rigid organization, and unbelievable stubbornness, all stitched together with the most dangerous ingredient known in the development of anything—secrecy.

The success of the German U-boat in World War I brought the torpedo from the realm of threat to the realm of reality. The mechanical shark could tear at the innards of any ship afloat and, generally, a ship torpedoed was a ship sunk. But the 1920s and the 1930s were still the age of the great guns and ships of the line. Modern battleships were equipped with rifles that could hurl one-ton projectiles to distances up to 20 miles. They were the backbone of the fleet and the center of naval thought.

The ship designers countered the ever-growing challenge of the big guns with careful compartmentation, thicker and tougher armor, and finally "blisters" to cushion the side armor from attack by torpedoes. But they could not do much about the bottom, where the mass of the surrounding water would focus a blast upward, lifting the ship bodily and breaking her back. Would it not be a great idea to design a torpedo to pass under the target ship and blast upward through her bottom?

The Navy Torpedo Station at Newport, Rhode Island, got to work and designed an exploder that reacted to the distortion of the earth's magnetic field caused by the steel of the ship's hull. The depth of the torpedo could be set to pass about five feet beneath the target's keel and when the magnetic influence hit maximum as the torpedo passed under the target, the exploder would trigger the warhead. In the case where the depth setting was too shallow and the torpedo actually collided with the hull, a second feature, actuated by sudden deceleration, would set off the warhead. Thus, this wonderful device offered the best of all worlds—the torpedo could be set to hit or it could be set to miss, and it would get the target in either case.

In greatest secrecy, and using the rapidly evolving components of the growing electronics industry, the Torpedo Station developed mechanisms, ran component tests, and finally built a prototype exploder. In 1926, the hulk of a submarine was towed out to sea as a target, a live torpedo equipped with the new exploder was fired under its keel, a huge explosion broke the ship in two, and it sank in deep water. The exploder was put into production as the Navy's secret Mk-6 exploder, but held in reserve for war use only, while a mechanically identical exploder, containing a contact mechanism, but not the magnetic device, was issued to the fleet as the Mk-5 exploder. The Mk-6 was never again tested in a live torpedo against a real target or issued for service tests in operating ships before the outbreak of World War II.

The Torpedo Station took its orders from the Torpedo Desk at the Bureau of Ordnance in the main Navy building on Constitution Avenue in Washington. The officer who occupied this powerful position, usually a commander or junior captain, was the czar of torpedoes. The existence and characteristics of the Mk-6 exploder were real military secrets and had to be held closely. Only a small portion of the mostly civilian Torpedo Station staff and a few key officers in the Bureau of Ordnance and the Office of the Chief of Naval Operations even knew of its existence.

At the same time, the Navy was developing a new family of torpedoes for its new ships and aircraft: the Mk-13 for use by aircraft which needed the lightest possible weapon, but didn't need much range; the Mk-14 for use by submarines, which had to be handled and serviced in very confined spaces and would be fired from underwater tubes; and the Mk-15 for use by destroyers, which had to be rugged enough to be fired from above water tubes and hit the water broadsides— it needed as much range as possible. The Mk-6 exploder was bulky and heavy, weighing over 100 pounds, so these torpedoes were designed to accommodate it, and the Mk-5 exploder was beefed up to equal its weight as well as its size.

As time passed and the war approached, the fleet commanders and certain small groups at their headquarters were informed of the new exploder and stocks were assembled at key locations. The bombs had hardly stopped falling at Pearl Harbor when special teams went to each ship and squadron to remove the Mk-5s and install the Mk-6s in all fleet torpedoes.

The first submarine war patrols were disappointing. A number of fish were fired, but very few targets sunk. Returning skippers were sure their fish had run hot, straight, and normal right to the target, but older heads chalked it up to inexperience. Some skippers saw explosions at the target waterline, but the ship sailed on. They began to suspect the warheads were "prematuring"—exploding just before they arrived at the target. It could be that the fish were running too deep, not close enough to the hull for the magnetic detector. CinCUS, himself a submariner, became interested and ordered Mk-14s to be fired through sub-merged nets to determine the actual depths at which they were running. On 1 August 1942, the submarine commands were informed of a 10-foot error in depth performance of the Mk-14, but nothing for the other Marks.

At Midway, three squadrons of torpedo planes carried their Mk-13s to the enemy and only a handful of planes returned. They were the most skilled and best-trained torpedo pilots America had, yet they scored no hits. The failure was credited to swarms of Zeros, obsolete aircraft, and bad luck, but officialdom never questioned why the half dozen deadly torpedoes, released so close aboard their chosen targets that the victim could not dodge, produced no results.

The battle testing of the destroyer weapon didn't commence until Savo became a common name. At the first battle, *Bagley*'s full salvo at Mikawa's column with no results was shrugged off as fired too late to have a chance. Two months later, *Duncan*'s solo drive toward Goto's flagship was remembered for the burning hulk that staggered out of the battle, not the two desperate torpedo shots she got off at *Furutaka* at less than a mile. After another month, on the night of the fateful Friday the thirteenth, *Barton* got off four torpedoes to no observable effect before she went down; *Cushing* fired six fish at *Hiei* 1,000 yards away and thought three of them were bull's-eyes, but they had no effect on the big ship and might have pre-matured; *Laffey* got off two torpedoes at the battle-wagon at point-blank range and saw them bounce off her blisters before she was shattered by gunfire and torpedoed herself; *Sterett* fired a salvo of four torpedoes at the leviathan from a perfect 2,000 yards, but nothing happened; *O'Bannon* added two more and saw their wakes ribbon straight to the target, but there was no explosion; *Monssen* got a five-fish spread off at *Hiei* from 4,000 yards and another at a fast-moving target on her beam, but she saw no explosions from her efforts; *Fletcher* fired her 10 torpedoes in a deliberate attack by radar from 7,000 yards after the melee had calmed down and observed a gratifying glow in the sky in the direction of the target, but no more—*Hiei*'s critical wound was from a cruiser's shell into her steering gear room and *Kirishima* wasn't touched during the battle.

Two nights later the four American destroyers were shattered by gunfire before they got a good torpedo shot at the various Japanese attackers and only *Gwin* expended any torpedoes during the battle—the shock of shells hitting her amidships severed the holdback pins in her torpedo tubes and some of her fish slid harmlessly into the sea. Next day when it became evident that *Benham* couldn't make it and *Gwin* was ordered to sink her, four Mk-15 torpedoes were fired at her at short range with no results—*Gwin* had to sink her with gunfire.

Even the carrier battle of the Santa Cruz Islands dropped hints about the shortcomings of the Mk-15 torpedo. While stopped to rescue a downed American pilot, *Porter* was hit by a torpedo. During a lull in the battle, when it was decided *Porter* could not be saved, *Shaw* was assigned the job of dispatching her. Two torpedoes fired at ideal range passed under the stricken ship with no effect. *Shaw* had to sink her with 5-inch gunfire. That same evening when it was decided to sink the crippled *Hornet,* destroyers *Mustin* and *Anderson* each fired eight fish

at short range into the crippled hull with little effect. They then tried, unsuccess-
fully, to put her under with 5-inch projectiles.

That something was terribly wrong shouted out from the pages of the ago-
nized battle reports, but the elaborate and compartmented staffs continued to
grind out self-serving paragraphs about radios or inflammables, and the head
of the Torpedo Desk stood firm. The admirals criticized anything that didn't
remind them of their days in the four-pipers, but left ordnance to the experts. In
the end the fault was assigned to the users of the torpedoes without recognizing
that the problem lay in the weapon itself. CinCPac called for better training and
more torpedo practices—instead of demanding that the chief of the Bureau of
Ordnance get those damned torpedoes fixed.

Of course, a failure of the magnetic feature of the Mk-6 could be avoided
by inactivating the magnetic feature and shooting to hit. For the operators to
decide to do so would be a bitter pill for the Mk-6 inventors at Newport, who
firmly believed they had produced the most deadly weapon ever provided to the
sailor. Soon many submarine captains refused to rely on the wonderful magnetic feature and used only the contact setting, but this did not seem to solve
the problem, in fact, not even half of it. Sometimes the torpedoes exploded as
planned, but often, particularly when used in the perfect beam shot, they failed
to explode. The captains complained, the admirals questioned, but the Bureau
of Ordnance held firm in its conviction that the Mk-14 was a good torpedo with
a good exploder.

And there was good reason for the Torpedo Station to have faith in its product—it was the most thoroughly tested weapon in the Navy's arsenal. Every
torpedo delivered to the fleet had made one or more successful test runs on the
test range at Newport or at Keyport, Washington, and its correct performance
could be proved by referring to the records. The log which accompanied each
torpedo as it made its way to the fleet gave complete details of each element of its
performance while it was being ranged.

On the 24th of July 1943, nearly eight months after the battle of Tassafaronga, the U.S. Submarine *Tinosa* winged an ex–whale factory ship, *Tonan Maru*,
of almost 20,000 tons, which was being used as a Japanese tanker, bringing the
huge ship to a stop with a torpedo hit near her stern. *Tinosa* then maneuvered to
an ideal position about 1,000 yards on the big ship's beam to administer the coup
de grace. One after another, she fired eight torpedoes directly against the side of
the monster, could hear them hit, but got no explosions. Upon return to Pearl,

the skipper, Lieutenant Commander L. R. "Dan" Daspit, went straight to Rear Admiral Lockwood, ComSubPac, and demanded action. He got it.

First, Lockwood sent a submarine to sea to fire two carefully prepared torpedoes directly into the deep cliffs on the south side of Kahoolawe. One exploded but the other did not. The dud was recovered and showed that the firing pin had been released on impact, but it did not fire the detonator.

Next he had a tower built ashore and released torpedoes equipped with Mk-6 exploders and booster charges, but no other explosives, to drop 90 feet nose-first onto a steel plate to duplicate the impact with which a torpedo hits the side of a ship. Seven out of ten booster charges did not explode—the friction caused by the instantaneous deceleration was too great for the firing pin spring to drive the pin home. Additional experiments revealed that in a glancing blow, such as the *Tinosa* shot that hit the *Tonan Maru* near the stern, the firing pin could work. It was the occasional success achieved with a glancing blow that kept the fire of faith kindled in the hearts of the diehards at Newport. It was a faith that contributed to the death of thousands of sailors and airmen during the long struggle of World War II.

In an otherwise amusing quirk of fate, Professor Albert Einstein had been shown the design of the Mk-6 at the beginning of the war and shocked the proud naval officer showing him the Navy's best kept secret by telling him it would not work. He even took the time to send a note next day, containing a sketch of a crushable structure that could be added to the nose of the torpedo to moderate the deceleration and give the firing pin spring a chance to do its job.

But on the 30th of November 1942, Cole's four destroyers had their Mk-15s equipped with Mk-6 exploders and they set their torpedoes to run under the target's keel as instructed by ComDesPac.

In a test firing on a torpedo range or during a normal torpedo practice firing by an operational ship, the warhead with its exploder was removed from the torpedo and an exercise head installed in its place. This exercise head contained any instrumentation needed to record the performance of the torpedo and was filled with water to simulate the weight of the explosive. At the end of the run, when the torpedo's fuel was exhausted, compressed air blew this water out and the resulting buoyancy brought the torpedo to the surface where it could be recovered, cleaned up, and made ready for use again.

In the fleet, ships trained in the preparation and use of torpedoes by firing their own service torpedoes at each other. The torpedo was, of course, equipped with only a non-explosive exercise head and was set to pass safely under the target ship's keel. To hit the friendly target's hull with a ton and a half torpedo going at 45 knots could seriously damage the ship, so any adjustments were always slanted toward the safe side—to ensure the torpedo ran deep enough.

In 1938, a division of destroyers off San Diego reported that their torpedoes were running deep, having surfaced with their exercise heads covered with mud from the bottom in 90 feet of water. The officer BuOrd sent out to investigate blamed the event on rough handling and poor maintenance by the destroyer-men. The same year, Newport was having a terrible time trying to develop the proper speed-altitude combination for the TBD torpedo plane to drop the Mk-13 torpedo—the torpedoes kept digging into the bottom of Narragansett Bay!

The depth at which a torpedo is running can be easily determined by firing it through a net and measuring the distance from the surface to the hole the torpedo makes, but Newport didn't like the idea. Nets were crude and cumbersome. In a current, they couldn't be depended upon to hang straight down from their moorings. Newport preferred measuring the torpedo's depth with a recording barograph carried in the practice head.

Using a barograph to record the torpedo's depth vs. time was a great idea, particularly since it could be used for every practice torpedo shot at sea without having to worry about nets. The only trouble was that measuring depth was not quite that simple. The designers forgot about Professor Bernouilli's theorem. The pressure seen at an orifice in the side of a torpedo is the pressure induced by the weight of water above it reduced by an amount dependent on the square of the velocity of the water flowing past the orifice. The velocity of flow past the orifice would normally be expected to be equal to the speed of the torpedo through the water, but, depending on the location of the opening along the body of the torpedo and particularly the form of the structure around the opening, the velocity could be greater or less than that of the torpedo. The result was that a torpedo had to run deeper than desired for the pressure at the orifice leading to the depth mechanism to equal that measured statically for the depth set. The faster the torpedo moved through the water, the deeper it had to go to satisfy the pressure setting.

Thus the elaborate testing of U.S. torpedoes was flawed in several aspects. The explosive performance of the warhead against the hulls of various types of ships had not been tested, the operation of the Mk-6 exploder had not been verified against these hulls or under the various magnetic conditions which would be encountered, and finally, the depth performance of the torpedo was being measured by an instrument, which was itself measuring the depth inaccurately.

Although the dramatic action by Rear Admiral Lockwood revealed the faults of the Mk-6 exploder in the late summer of 1943, the true situation concerning the depth performance of the Mk-15 torpedo and its sisters was not determined until the spring of 1944 when wind tunnel tests demonstrated that the pressure being seen at the orifice of the depth mechanism was much different from that which was expected, because of the flow pattern around the torpedo. Admiral Blandy of BuOrd initiated a thorough testing program for torpedoes and undertook a vigorous program to correct the flaws and to produce a new generation of improved torpedoes. Unfortunately, the critical battles of the Pacific had already been fought.

The reader might also wonder why the U.S. Navy had done nothing about so obvious a solution to torpedo propulsion as substituting pure oxygen for air. In fact, the Torpedo Station at Newport had been busy with such a development during the 1920s, and in 1931 actually "ranged" a prototype oxygen torpedo. Unfortunately the motor burned out and the controls jammed. There was also a damaging fire in the development laboratory and funds in the early 1930s were very tight.

The U.S. Navy preferred hydrogen peroxide instead of pure oxygen because H_2O_2 was considered easier to handle. When sprayed on a catalyst it produced steam rich in free oxygen into which a fuel, such as diesel oil, could be sprayed, producing a very energetic product. The beauty of hydrogen peroxide was that it did not have to be kept at high pressure and its rate of decomposition was easily controlled. Newport dubbed its particular combination of ingredients Navol and in 1937 a Navol-powered Mk-14 torpedo ran 16,500 yards on the range at 46 knots. BuOrd started a program to build a Navol torpedo, the Mk-17, for destroyer use, with specifications calling for 16,000 yards at 50 knots and carrying a 600-pound warhead, but only six had been completed by 7 December 1941. This project was increased to produce a Mk-16 torpedo for submarine use, and by the end of the war Newport had produced about 1,000 Navol torpedoes.

~ X ~
THE GUNNERY PROBLEM

Radar was a great development that shaped much of World War II. In the Battle of Britain it permitted the detection of aircraft at long ranges so that defenses could be alerted, aircraft scrambled, and non-combatants gotten into shelters. It permitted defensive fighters to be vectored to intercept the incoming bombers long before they had reached their bomb release points. It also opened a new era where flight could be conducted safely at night and in bad weather. At sea in the Atlantic it forced the submarines to submerge and greatly reduced their effectiveness; in the Pacific it greatly improved the defenses of the carrier task forces and introduced a new ability to fight at night.

The first shipboard radar to enter service in the Pacific Fleet was the CXAM, a relatively low-frequency radar with an enormous "bedspring" antenna which could be carried by only the largest ships. It was a truly remarkable radar which could reliably detect incoming planes at ranges of about 75 miles. It had a broad beam and a slow rate of rotation, but it was very satisfactory as a warning device and, as the skill of the air controllers improved, it served well for intercepting incoming enemy planes. It was not very useful for detecting surface ships, however, because it had a significant blind angle at the surface due to its low frequency.

For smaller ships an SC radar of somewhat higher frequency was developed, but it was never in the class of the CXAM in performance or reliability. When in good working order, which in most ships was not often, it could detect aircraft out to about 60 miles and was occasionally useful in detecting surface targets.

The antennae of these early radars, mounted as high in the ship as practical, would slowly scan the horizon until the presence of a target was indicated by a blip on the horizontal range line traced on the face of the cathode-ray scope of the radar console. When the operator spotted a blip, he interrupted the antenna's motion and moved it back and forth across the bearing of the blip to find the center. Range was then measured by cranking a "range step" out to the target blip and reading the resulting range on a calibrated dial. Unfortunately, even with the large antennae, the angular beam width of these early radars was quite large, and significant amounts of energy were focused in other directions in side lobes. As a result, if a radar was close to land or a heavy rain squall, enough energy was received with the antenna trained in any direction to saturate the receiver and blank out the desired weaker targets within the range band of the land or weather "clutter."

As mentioned frequently in the preceding chapters, the first radar developed for detecting surface ships at sea, the SG radar, was a dramatic leap forward. Operating at a much higher frequency than the air search radars, its beam width was a narrow 3° and its side lobes negligible. Most importantly, it scanned rapidly at one complete horizon search every four seconds and displayed its echoes on its PPI, scope with "own ship" in the center and targets displayed at their true bearings and relative range. Set on long range, the scope could show targets out to 75,000 yards; at short range, out to 15,000 yards. The special coating on the PPI screen glowed long enough so that returns from one sweep lasted until refreshed by the next sweep, so a continuous picture was displayed. For the first time, the sailor had a bird's-eye view of the sea around him, day or night.

But even the SG had shortcomings. Its 3° beam width still exaggerated narrow targets and smeared them into nearby neighbors, but the biggest disadvantage was that to measure range accurately, the steady rotation had to be interrupted while the antenna was scanned back and forth to find the center of the target and the range measured on an adjacent range scope. This took several seconds for each target, so the SG picture was lost each time an accurate range or bearing was needed.

Fire control radars had to solve a different set of problems. By the beginning of World War II, the science of naval gunnery was reaching its all-time peak. Huge rifled gun barrels were produced at the Naval Gun Factory in Washington to the tightest of tolerances, mounted in armored turrets or unarmored

Reduced gun flash produced by using "flashless" powder. USS Nicholas *(DD-449) in battle off Vella Lavella, 18 August 1943. Photo from National Archives.*

gun mounts, which were packed with powerful mechanisms to load the guns and to lay them in elevation and train. The older units depended on the pointer and trainer matching pointers to follow the synchro signals from the director—later models could be shifted into automatic and the operators just watched. Corrections for ballistics, air density, own ship's course, roll and pitch, target course and speed, and a host of other esoteric errors were calculated in a marvelous electro-mechanical rangekeeper and added to the raw signals from the director to produce gun train order and gun elevation order. Excellent optics in the directors enabled accurate observation of the target and precise measurement of elevation and bearing, but the measurement of range was more difficult.

Range had traditionally been measured with binocular rangefinders, which reached a length of 40 feet between lenses in battleship installations, but the accuracy was never reliable enough because of atmospherics and operator errors. In addition, they could not be used in low visibility or at night. Radar suddenly promised ranges accurate within a few feet and could be used in the black of night. Radar for gunnery had every bit as much promise as radar for air control, so the designers at BuOrd got busy. In late 1941, strange snowplow-shaped antennae began to appear on the main battery directors of cruisers and other heavies as the surface-fire FC radar made its appearance. By the spring of 1942, along with fleetwide installations of the SC, it was followed by what appeared to be two FC antennas, one on top of the other, hung on the rangefinders of dual-purpose directors in all combatants. This was the FD radar, which could not only track a target in range and bearing, it could also track an aircraft in elevation. Night, fog, rain, or snow lost their power to blind the gunner.

To eliminate the "clutter" which might saturate its receiver and cause the automatic circuits to reduce sensitivity, the fire control radars could switch into a range-gate mode, where the reflected signals were displayed only during the time when echoes were expected from the vicinity of the selected target. The range-gate was usually set at 500 or 1,000 yards, with the target notch in the center, to allow observation of the fall of shot and permit corrections to be made while the target was being tracked. Shorter range-gates could be selected, particularly for AA fire, but any shots falling outside of the gate were not visible. A range operator manned the master console of the FC or FD, and with a hand crank kept the target pip in the center of the notch to measure range, which was automatically transmitted to the rangekeeper. The improvement in range accuracy and the ability to spot the fall of shot was phenomenal.

For radar tracking in bearing or elevation, the radar antennae were divided electrically into two parts, each pointing slightly off the line-of-sight to the target. The radar transmitted alternately from either side of the antenna at a rate of about a thousand times per second, and the returns were displayed on a scope available to the director pointer or trainer. The return of all target reflections within the range-gate from both sides of the antenna was displayed simultaneously on the operator's scope, with the return from one side slightly delayed from that of the other to separate the traces. The pointer or trainer moved the director to keep the height of the returns from the two sides equal.

The FC and FD were quite effective for firing at single targets in a clear environment. When two targets were found in the range-gate at the same time, however, the operators tended to split the difference and point the director between the targets. The return echoes in the range-gate were also quite irregular as the target rolled and pitched or otherwise changed aspect, and there was little correlation between a ship's appearance to the eye and what it looked like on the radar. Keeping the height of the pips equal wasn't easy. It was like watching worms squirm and trying to respond to their movements. Shell splashes added extra targets in the range-gate, tempting the operator to chase the splashes.

For initially finding a target in the presence of others, the fire control radars were poor substitutes for the radars designed for searching. Not much could be seen to distinguish a valid target from almost any other type of clutter until the range-gate had been slewed to the target, and the trainer had nothing to go on until the pip was within the gate. Normally, the director was coached to a target from data obtained by a search radar.

The preferred method of firing was to use radar for range and to use optics for bearing and elevation. Using optics, the pointer and trainer could normally keep the crosshairs steadily on the target—when tracking by radar, however, the crosshairs would often wander back and forth across the target, sometimes wandering a full ship length away. Should the target become obscured for some reason, the pointer or trainer could shift to matching pips by just taking his eyes from the telescope and looking at the small radar scope next to it. The radar was consequently considered a stand-by system for bearing and elevation.

But all the guns, fire control, and radar were of no use if the ammunition wasn't effective. Projectiles were carefully designed and machined to meet very exacting tolerances. The weight and aerodynamic drag had to be precise for every class of projectile, and there were many. Major-caliber guns had to be provided with armor-piercing projectiles that could punch through the protective armor and explode within the enemy ship. This led to specially hardened blunt-nosed projectiles, tipped with softer metal and streamlined with a windshield to help the projectile dig in instead of bouncing off when hitting the enemy's face-hardened plates. The fuze had to be rugged enough to stand the impact and delay the explosion until the projectile had passed through the armor. All this left only a little room for high explosives, so for other than armor-piercing, a common projectile was provided, which carried much more explosive and was designed to add hundreds of lethal fragments to the power of the blast.

For anti-aircraft use by the 5-inch batteries a common type projectile was provided, which had a mechanical time fuze (MTF) in its nose which could be set for the number of seconds (in hundredths) predicted for its flight to the target. The 5-inch star shell was similar to the AA common, but when its MTF triggered, it blew out of its base a magnesium flare attached to a small parachute. The flare ignited upon ejection and would burn for a couple of minutes as it descended slowly to the surface, shedding a brilliant white light as it fell.

But one of the most important ingredients in gunnery is the propellant, and the U.S. Navy was rightly proud of its smokeless powder, used for guns large and small. It produced high energy, was very stable, was much less sensitive than the famous British cordite, and produced only a very small amount of light smoke. It did, however, produce a blinding flash when fired.

From the beginning, the disadvantage of the bright flash during a night engagement was recognized, but the other advantages of the safe and efficient powder outweighed this one disadvantage. Memories of the explosion and loss of the *Maine* in the Spanish-American War and the loss of the British battle cruisers at Jutland haunted the Navy safety experts. Magazine explosions were not just a disadvantage, they were fatal. Of all of the candidate propellant powders, smokeless was considered the most resistant to impact or fire, so all other considerations took second place. Although the flash could be greatly reduced by introducing substances which produced thick smoke, the disadvantages of such powder in daylight actions outweighed the promised advantage at night.

In following the rather elaborate discussion of the gunfire of the individual ships in this engagement, it might be helpful to tabulate the firepower available on each ship. The guns of the ships of Task Force Sixty-Seven at Tassafaronga were as indicated in Figure 4, on the following page.

Figure 4. *The major guns of the ships of Task Force Sixty-Seven.*

SHIP	GUNS		MAX RANGE	RATE OF FIRE
	No.	Size	Yards	Shots/Min.
Minneapolis	9	8-inch/55	29,000	4
	8	5-inch/25	15,000	15
New Orleans	9	8-inch/55	29,000	4
	8	5-inch/25	15,000	15
Pensacola	10	8-inch/55	29,000	4
	8	5-inch/25	15,000	15
Northampton	9	8-inch/55	29,000	4
	8	5-inch/25	15,000	15
Honolulu	15	6-inch/47	25,000	10
	8	5-inch/38	18,300	15
Fletcher	5	5-inch/38	18,300	15
Perkins	4	5-inch/38	18,300	15
Maury	4	5-inch/38	18,300	15
Drayton	4	5-inch/38	18,300	15
Lamson	4	5-inch/38	18,300	15
Lardner	4	5-inch/38	18,300	15

The reader may be surprised at this briefing in naval gunnery, but it is offered to help in understanding what did happen and what did not happen at Tassafaronga. In naval warfare, the organization of the fleet, the selection of commanders, the strategies employed, and the maneuvers of the ships are all for the purpose of bringing one's weapons into position to destroy the enemy. These weapons must work as planned, or the entire undertaking is for naught. The Battle of Tassafaronga was an unusually revealing testing ground for the weapons of both sides. More than a test of strategy and tactics, it was a weapons test.

─◦ XI ◦─
ANALYSIS &
CRITIQUE

After reading all of the available action reports from the ships and commanders involved in the Battle of Tassafaronga, one has a new appreciation of the term "fog of battle." How could such distorted views of factual events be held by serious observers? The players, reporters, and critics on both sides were mature professionals, conducting the business of war with the greatest of dedication. How could they report events that did not happen? How could they so grossly misinterpret the things they saw?

The shortcomings which confused and hampered the American side were not the obvious imperfections of a great nation scrambling to organize its defenses, like lack of training, unit integrity, or frequent changes of commanders. The critical shortcomings were built into the U.S. Navy over a period of years, beginning long before the tragedy of Pearl Harbor. Defective torpedoes, poor intelligence, blinding gunfire, and overconfidence all played their part, but how could the observers on the scene be so wrong in reporting what happened? The answer lies in the human mind and the human heart.

In the staccato glimpses each man caught of the unfolding drama, he saw what he expected to see, what he hoped to see. The commanders knew they were intercepting a re-supply mission and reconnaissance had reported transports, so they saw transports. Cruisers expected to fight cruisers and had little fear of destroyers, so cruiser men saw cruisers. Gunners knew the lethality of their guns, so when the blast of their salvoes subsided and there was no target, they were sure it had sunk or been blown away. The shock of one's own ship firing is very impressive, so one is led to equate volume of fire with effectiveness of fire. The captains listened to many stories, but they heard what they wanted to hear and so reported.

To discover how the final official report, whittled down by successive commands, told the commander in chief that four enemy destroyers had been sunk and two or more others damaged, when only one ship, *Takanami,* had been seriously wounded, the author obtained from the Navy Historical Center's Operational Archives copies of the action reports of every U.S. ship and command which took part in the engagement. He also obtained a copy of the Japanese report on the battle. Admiral Tanaka's personal account of the entire Solomons campaign as well as this particular battle was available from Naval Institute publications. From these sources he plotted, on a scale of 1,000 yards to the inch, the navigational tracks of the U.S. ships, the ranges and bearings of all targets they fired upon, and any significant sightings reported. There were a few inconsistencies among the sources, but by carefully plotting all reported data and modifying one or two bearings to fit reality, the time-phased pattern of the battle emerged. He filled the gaps in the very meager ship movement data of the Japanese battle report, sticking exactly to all times and actions reported, by drawing on his own experience in destroyers and cruisers and the known characteristics of the ships involved. He dared to postulate what the various Japanese captains would have done under the circumstances and he also invented the name "Shimamoto" for Tanaka's flag captain, since the records available did not provide the identity of this key officer.

The tracks of the Japanese torpedoes were constructed by connecting a known hit on an American ship with a reported time of firing by a Japanese ship combined with the 49-knot speed of a Type 93 torpedo to determine its source. The positions of the beached transports were derived from the location of submerged wrecks shown on the current navigational charts. A summary track chart of the action is shown in Figure 5 and the two most critical 5-minute periods are shown in Figures 6 and 7.

Certainly Admiral Wright and Admiral Kinkaid planned for the battle as well as any humans could. Their plan for night action in Op-Plan 1-42 fitted the actual encounter perfectly, covering every essential aspect of the battle. Perhaps they had planned too well and Admiral Wright had thought too much. He was certainly concentrating on the essential mission, of thwarting the re-supply of the Japanese troops ashore and had made up his mind before the battle started to bore in and get those transports. His pre-action message outlining his battle intentions put Cole on notice that he might not allow time for the torpedoes to reach their target before opening gunfire. But why? What was the hurry? If there was going to be a significant reinforcement as he expected, it would take several hours to unload the ships and he would have plenty of time to deal with relatively slow transports. The author's guess is that he hoped to catch the enemy cruisers and destroyers by surprise and deal with the transports later. He also had little confidence that a surprise could be delivered by his destroyers ahead and preferred to rely on his cruisers' guns.

Wright and all of his cruiser captains believed that he had kept them out of torpedo waters, so he might be forgiven for pressing in a bit closer than his planned 12,000 yards, but why did he not turn away to control the range as he stated in his plan? More importantly, why did he not simply reverse course to really foil any incoming torpedoes; even American torpedoes could reach 10,000 yards. Despite his concern about restricted waters, Iron Bottom Bay is a big body of water, certainly big enough to allow a lot of tactical maneuvering. If there had been enemy cruisers or battleships, as had been experienced in every previous battle, he would have been much better off standing off at 15,000 yards or more and capitalizing on the anticipated American superiority in gunnery and radar.

The only valid reason for Wright to have withheld permission for Cole to fire his torpedoes would have been that the identity of the target was in doubt. That was never an issue. Cole, thoroughly familiar with his SG radar and his torpedoes, planned to stay outside the limit of visibility, estimated by others to have been about 4,000 to 6,000 yards that night, and hit the enemy before he was even aware of the presence of the firing destroyers. He executed his plan skillfully. If Wright did not like Cole's approach, it was too late to change it—the die had been cast. So Wright's second-guessing of his subordinate resulted in a critical delay of five minutes, which left *Fletcher* with a much longer, overtaking shot and required shifting the torpedoes to low speed. It also changed *Perkins'* intermediate speed shot to a less favorable one, although it did not hinder *Drayton*'s long-range effort.

Wright's order to commence fire less than a minute after he had released his torpedoes demolished any hope of the fish catching the Japanese off guard, but as things turned out in the first frantic minutes of the battle, several of them managed to maneuver into harm's way. Until the lead destroyers opened fire with their guns after Wright's general order, there is no evidence in the Japanese reports that they were even aware of the presence of these four ships.

Wright gave only two significant orders during the entire engagement. The first was to prevent Cole from firing and the second was his "commence firing" to all ships. He ordered no tactical maneuvers at all in the period from 2314, when he turned to 300°, until 2328, when his flagship had her bow blown off and his TBS was knocked out. Before opening fire, he obviously believed that his ships could not be seen by the enemy units being tracked by his radars. Even after he was hit, he could not believe he had been torpedoed by any of the surface ships he was engaging.

As the two forces approached each other, an understandable mistake on the American side was to presume that the enemy ships were in a set formation, that all ships were going on the same course and speed. When the order to commence fire was given, just after 2320, *Takanami* had slowed to perhaps 10 knots to maintain her sentinel position to seaward, *Kawakaze* and *Suzukaze* were dead in the water off Doma with their boats in the water, *Naganami* was moving ahead to back up *Takanami,* and Sato had led his four ships past *Takanami* and was making 30 knots toward Tassafaronga. Most American ships tracked only *Takanami,* which was the closest target most of the time, and had averaged her speed as she slowed.

Takanami had been watching the approaching column for eight minutes when she was taken under fire, so she was certainly ready to fire her torpedoes. As the American shells fell around him and moved closer, Captain Ogura undoubtedly knew he had to act and, about two minutes after the first American shell landed, he probably fired a full salvo of eight torpedoes at the head of the American column. It was a stroke of luck that he hit both *Minneapolis* and *New Orleans* with the same salvo, but with only 30 seconds between the times the two ships were struck, there was hardly time for two separately fired half-salvoes. With a 6,500-yard torpedo run and 1° between fish, the geometry fits nicely. Such a spread would also have hit at least one American ship had it been aimed by *Takanami* at any other point down the long column.

Takanami opened fire with her guns almost as soon as the lead cruisers commenced firing, and Tanaka reported seeing hits on the first salvo. Since no shells hit any of our cruisers, or even came close, what Tanaka observed must have been the cruisers' 5-inch batteries firing star shells—the flashes would have appeared different from the massive flames belching from the turrets. It is also interesting that all Japanese reports speak of aircraft flares being used abundantly by the Americans, but the only aircraft flare dropped came much later. The Japanese were apparently unacquainted with star shells.

Takanami was pummeled by gunfire from *Minneapolis, New Orleans, Northampton, Perkins,* and *Maury* in the first few minutes of the engagement. According to the author's analysis, she was fired at with guns or torpedoes at one time or another by every ship in the task force including *Lamson,* which used her as the point of aim for most of her star shells. She was heavily damaged, set afire, and brought to a halt. Although she had numerous explosions topside, some of which were probably her re-load torpedoes, she did not sink. In fact, she floated in her pitiful condition for the next three hours before she went under. She was certainly a remarkably damage-resistant ship. Apparently, her magazines never exploded.

Working down the American column from head to tail, *Fletcher* fired her first half-salvo at *Takanami* and *Kuroshio,* lined up one behind the other. The torpedoes missed ahead of *Takanami* because she had been hit, slowed radically, and turned right before they arrived, and *Kuroshio,* at 30 knots, passed clear before they ever reached her. *Fletcher*'s second torpedo half-salvo was aimed at *Kagero,* but with target speed set at 15 knots and Sato's ships making 30 knots or more, they also did not have a chance until Captain Sato graciously reversed course and almost collided with them. As the plot shows, at 2334 all four ships of Sato's group were in the vicinity of *Fletcher*'s torpedoes. Of course, even if the torpedoes had passed under their keels, there is little chance that they would have exploded.

Fletcher fired 60 rounds of 5-inch at *Kuroshio* under full radar control with her FD, but the target angle was deep on the quarter and the target was running at twice the speed radar plot had reported. No shells hit *Kuroshio,* and the FD range-gate was empty when fire was checked. *Fletcher*'s gunners and lookouts were blinded by the increasing number of star shells falling between her and the enemy, and she was unable to find another target.

Perkins fired a full spread of eight torpedoes at *Takanami,* but they passed ahead because *Takanami* came to a stop. *Naganami,* coming up from astern, however, surged into the area covered by the spread, made a tight U-turn, and was headed out when the torpedoes arrived. Tanaka reported he saw torpedo wakes just ahead, so some of the torpedoes could have passed under his flagship, but did no damage, probably because they were running too deep. *Perkins*

Figure 5. *Summary track chart and torpedo fire.*

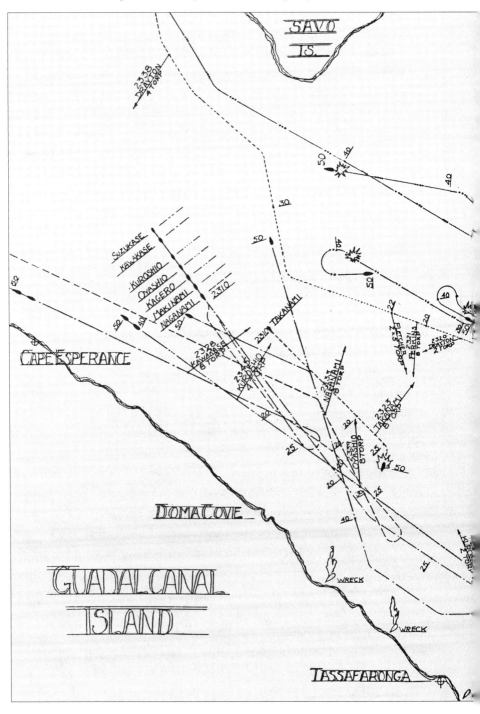

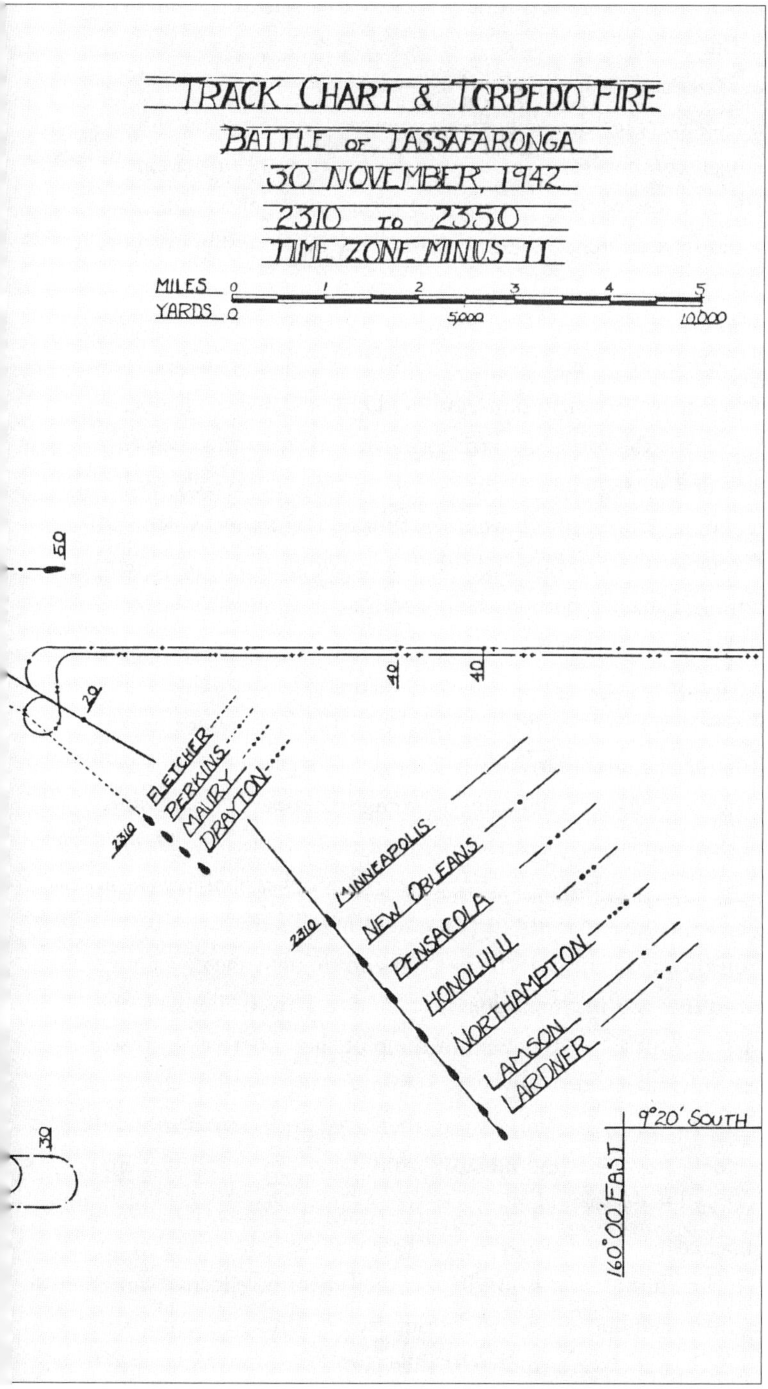

TRACK CHART & TORPEDO FIRE

BATTLE OF TASSAFARONGA

30 NOVEMBER, 1942

2310 TO 2350

TIME ZONE MINUS 11

MILES 0 1 2 3 4 5
YARDS 0 5,000 10,000

50

20

40 40

FLETCHER
PERKINS
MAURY
DRAYTON

2310

MINNEAPOLIS
NEW ORLEANS
PENSACOLA
HONOLULU
NORTHAMPTON
LAMSON
LARDNER

2310

30

9°20' SOUTH

160°00' EAST

pounded *Takanami* with 50 rounds of 5-inch and may very well have inflicted critical damage, but as *Takanami*'s turn put the lead destroyers astern, she was concealed in smoke and spray.

Maury fired her twenty 5-inch salvoes at *Takanami* without doubt, but there is no way of knowing whether they hit. Her target was concealed by smoke, which could have been coming from *Takanami*'s gunfire forward or her smoke generator aft. In any case, the wind was variously reported as about 6 knots from the east, which would have stretched the smoke from the burning ship as a curtain between the two forces.

Drayton obviously had the best SG radar of all the ships and she concentrated on distant *Kawakaze* and *Suzukaze,* lying-to off Doma. Unfortunately, she did not have the courage of her convictions and fired only two fish at these easy targets. As the plot shows, the torpedoes arrived in time to embarrass *Suzukaze* as she doubled back and passed close to her initial position, so severely in fact that she did not get her torpedoes off. *Drayton* also spotted *Naganami,* which had been missed by *Fletcher*'s radar, and treated her to a hundred rounds of 5-inch, all under radar control. Tanaka reported a hail of shells falling close aboard, but *Naganami* was not hit.

As for the incoming torpedo wakes reported by the last three ships of the lead destroyers, there were none possible during the period before Cole led his ships northward. As the star shells blossomed, they did indeed reveal the wakes of torpedoes, but they were the bubbles from outgoing torpedoes from the ships ahead. The author personally saw them and reported them as such to *Maury*'s bridge. The Japanese oxygen torpedo might cause enough phosphorescence in tropical waters to be seen, but it did not leave a trail of bubbles on the surface.

As for explosions from American torpedoes, *Perkins* thought she saw a large explosion on her target when her torpedoes would have arrived. Perhaps one of her torpedoes actually hit and exploded, but the plot shows her salvo missed *Takanami,* so it is more likely that any large explosion was from a Japanese re-load torpedo being set off by gunfire. As for other large explosions attributed to American torpedoes, they were undoubtedly from American warheads detonating as the torpedoes hit the reefs along the shore of Guadalcanal.

Minneapolis opened fire on *Takanami* and believed she had sunk her by the fourth salvo. As the illumination from the star shells became effective, some observers correctly identified her as a destroyer, but the captain and the gunnery officer saw only one stack and were convinced she was a transport. There was a large explosion aboard the target, after which it could no longer be seen. Since the target could not be found by radar either, it is probable that her FC radar had been drawn off the target by the numerous shell splashes from *Perkins* and *Maury,* which were coming in almost directly across the line of fire and were certainly landing in her range-gate. When *Minneapolis* checked fire to see the results, the destroyers had stopped firing, so there was nothing to be seen and nothing on the radar; ergo, the target had been sunk.

The next target for *Minneapolis* was *Kawakaze,* a bit to the right of *Takanami* and correctly identified as a destroyer. It was a beam shot at 10,500 yards, but the target was just beginning to move and build up speed. With the unavoidable lag in a rangekeeper solution, her salvoes would have landed astern of the accelerating destroyer, and since both *Kawakaze* and *Suzukaze* would have been in her range-gate, her four salvoes were probably pointed to land between them. The fourth salvo was reported to merge with that of another American cruiser hitting the target amidships and breaking it in two. The bow and stern were seen to rise out of the water and the ship disappeared. The author can offer no better explanation of this other than to suggest that a salvo falling short, but in line with the target, would blank the center of the ship and perhaps give the impression of the bow and stern rising from a broken hull. That she should disappear from sight can be explained by the fact that the *Kawakaze* and *Suzukaze* were just passing behind the smoke being carried by the wind from the burning *Takanami.*

Minneapolis's third target, *Naganami,* was correctly identified as a large destroyer or cruiser, but which was also being engaged by *Pensacola,* not *New Orleans.* She was treated to one salvo, a straddle, and then disappeared. About this time, *Naganami* reversed course in a sharp turn to the right, and if she was making smoke, as she almost certainly was, the smoke would have blanked her from being seen from *Minneapolis.* At this moment, *Takanami*'s first torpedo ripped off *Minneapolis*'s bow, quickly followed by the second hitting amidships. Though her 5-inch battery ceased firing, her main battery continued with two more 8-inch salvoes. Tanaka agreed to many near misses, but reported no hits.

New Orleans also opened fire on *Takanami* and identified her as a destroyer. After two salvoes, and recognizing that other ships were also engaging the same target, she reported seeing her target blow up and disappear. Her next target, plotted to be *Naganami,* was identified as an *Atago*-class cruiser and treated to three salvoes before being seen to explode—of course, Tanaka did not agree with this damage assessment, but he acknowledged explosions close aboard.

By this time, star shell illumination had reached its peak, with some of them well ashore over Guadalcanal, and *New Orleans* found a cargo ship close to the beach as her next target. After two salvoes, there was a tremendous explosion on board the target, and the ship continued to burn for some time. She spotted another cargo ship to the left and after two salvoes, it too exploded and burned.

The only possible explanation for these last two *New Orleans* targets is that they were two of the transports Tanaka ordered run aground on the night of the 14th of November. By chance, Sato's ships were just passing in front of them and they would certainly appear to be juicy targets to the TF 67 gunners, who would have had no knowledge that they were there. Although by this time they had been thoroughly worked over by aircraft from Henderson Field and by the destroyer *McCalla* on the 15th, they would have appeared in the pale light of star shells to be fully operational ships. The deeply penetrating 8-inch, armor-piercing projectiles would certainly have found some remaining explosives in their holds. *Minneapolis* exploding ahead and, half a minute later, having her own bow blown off, terminated *New Orleans*'s search for new targets.

Pensacola, lacking an SG, took a little time to find a target, but as soon as the illumination got bright enough, she settled her sights on *Naganami,* which she identified as a three-stack light cruiser, and took her under fire with full ten-gun salvoes from her four 8-inch turrets. After her fifth salvo, there was a large explosion on board the target and the ship disappeared (*Naganami*'s turn and smoke screen). She shifted right to a target she found with her FC (*Takanami*) and resumed fire. As she opened on this second target, it came out of an apparent smoke screen and she identified it as a *Mogami* or *Yubari* cruiser, because of a single stack, rather fat at the base. Her second salvo hit home, the ship disappeared, so *Pensacola* unloaded through the muzzle and looked for more targets. *Takanami*'s after stack might well have been shot off by this time, and there were no doubt explosions erupting aboard. Her disappearance (into her own smoke) is quite believable.

When *Minneapolis,* then *New Orleans,* were hit and burst into flames, *Pensacola* swung left to pass, but returned quickly to her former course of 300° T. As she passed in front of the flames she was recognized by the Japanese captains as a *Texas*-class battleship—thus becoming the center of attention. *Kuroshio*'s two torpedoes, fired as she was silhouetted, could have been the ones that did her in, despite a torpedo run of 18,000 yards. *Naganami, Kawakaze, Oyashio,* and *Kagero* immediately started their approaches to get her.

At 2333, *Pensacola* found a new target (*Naganami*) with her FC radar, closing rapidly from port. When the target reached 6,000 yards, she resumed the regular cadence of her salvo fire and, after her seventh salvo, at a range of 7,000 yards, the target disappeared and was judged to be destroyed. A few sweeps of her director found another target (*Suzukaze*) at 12,000 yards and soon the main battery rangekeeper showed it was making 32 knots and heading for home. She fired three full salvoes at it, saw some flashes, but could not be sure of hits (*Suzukaze* was not hit but was probably lobbing some shells at *Pensacola*). She fired a couple of star shells over a suspicious shadow to starboard, and *Honolulu* quickly identified herself. She saw some small splashes ahead and suddenly she was shattered by a torpedo hitting in her after engine room. From where had it come? Who had fired it?

As related above, *Kuroshio's* long shot could have done it. More likely would be *Kawakaze's* eight-torpedo spread, fired from an ideal position at a modest range on her port bow, or equally from *Naganami,* closer to her beam, upon whom she was firing—both Japanese ships fired at about the same time, 2333. *Pensacola* was an easy target for any of them, since she never varied her course or her speed and had been advertising her position with regular salvoes.

Honolulu was considered the star of the show, but she scarcely deserves the distinction. Her main battery plot kept an excellent chronological record of events, so there was little difficulty in following her actions. She selected her first target deliberately (*Naganami*), correctly identified it as a destroyer, and fired two ranging salvoes. Observing them to straddle at 9,000 yards, she unleashed the fury of her fifteen 6-inch guns in a crescendo of continuous fire, using a 100-yard "rocking ladder." Blinded by the star shells and hampered by smoke, most of her firing was controlled by the FC. After 30 seconds of murderous fire, she checked fire to observe the results. Hits were reported by the director, and the rangekeeper indicated target speed was decreasing. So was range. She resumed fire with another blast of 6-inch as the target speed dropped to zero and the range continued to decrease. About this time, the two ships ahead had been hit, and Captain Hayler brought *Honolulu* hard right and increased to 30 knots. As the big ship steadied on her new course, the gunners gave their target a final blizzard of 6-inch, but in a moment the two crippled cruisers blocked the line of fire and *Honolulu* checked fire, the last range having been 7,150 yards.

Everyone who observed *Honolulu's* firing was impressed by its intensity, particularly Admiral Wright and Admiral Tisdale. So was Admiral Tanaka, who could not believe that his flagship could survive under such a hail of shells. But the friendly star shells and *Honolulu*'s FC radar operators saved him. The smoke and glare from the star shells forced the *Honolulu* gunners to depend on the FC for train as well as range, and the water around *Naganami* was churning with shell splashes. Tanaka was astonished by what he saw—the incoming fire was in range, but missing in deflection, quite the contrary of what one would expect.

But *Honolulu*'s fire did not stay in range long—as the thunderous fire threw up tall columns of water short of the target, the FC operator averaged the return and chased his own fall of shot. The plot shows that the range from *Honolulu* to *Naganami* was actually increasing continuously during the firing, never decreasing. In addition, after reversing her course, *Naganami* passed behind *Takanami*, as seen from *Honolulu*. By the time of the third 30-second burst of continuous fire, *Honolulu* had shifted from *Naganami* to the already crippled *Takanami*. The rangekeeper tracking which showed *Naganami*'s speed dropping to zero was caused by the change in bearing as she reversed course combined with *Honolulu* chasing her own salvoes. Having no reason to suspect what had happened, *Honolulu* reported her first target "was observed to blow up and sink," and her second target was being hit "when fire was checked due to the target being obscured."

The most probable reason *Honolulu* was never fired at and escaped all damage was that she disappeared behind the two flaming cruisers, opened the range several thousand yards, and never fired her main battery again. She fired star shells intermittently until 2336, hoping to sight a target, but after that her guns were silent—and the "battleship" *Pensacola* had not yet been hit. Captain Hayler's high speed and radical maneuvering was also the most potentially effective action taken by any cruiser commander.

Northampton had just reached the knuckle of the column movement and come to the new course of 300° when the firing order was given. Her FC found a target to the left of the targets being engaged by the lead cruisers and she opened fire at 11,000 yards. As the illumination improved, she identified her target as a destroyer leading two light cruisers in column. Her gunnery coordinates check exactly with the position of *Takanami*, but her sighting could only be satisfied by Sato's three leading ships, 30° to the left. This is one of the inconsistencies mentioned above. It must be remembered that *Northampton* was later sunk and most written records went down with her, so that two different observations might be combined into one is not surprising. After an estimated nine full salvoes, her gunners were sure their target had been sunk. During the last of her salvoes, her

FC radar's range-gate had been kept full of shell splashes, from two other cruisers and two destroyers, so it would not be surprising that she had drifted off target and, when the splashes subsided, there was nothing there.

When the lead cruisers were hit and *Northampton* sheered right following *Honolulu*'s lead, she checked fire to avoid endangering friendly ships. At 2336, after she had come back to course and had an open field of fire between *Pensacola* and the burning ships, she picked up *Naganami* and methodically gave her nine more salvoes. Her controlling director reported seeing the target explode and sink, but the author can offer no explanation for this observation. It is quite probable, however, that her FC radar had begun to fade, so when she checked fire to observe, she could see nothing visually against Guadalcanal in the background and her FC could no longer pick up a destroyer at the 12,000-yard range. Nevertheless, her captain reported with satisfaction that his guns had sunk two destroyers during the action and he was also sure he had seen an enemy light cruiser (*Takanami*) explode at a shorter range.

The report of sighting two torpedoes coming in from ahead of *Northampton* at 2348 cannot be explained, but Captain Kitts believed they were there and reported ordering "full right rudder." No Japanese torpedoes could have been coming from the west because there had been no Japanese ships in that direction to fire them. The Japanese oxygen torpedoes, leaving little or no wake, were not sighted by *Minneapolis* or *New Orleans* before they were hit, and it is unlikely that they would have been seen by *Northampton*. There is no doubt, however, that *Northampton* was ripped open and set afire with a tremendous explosion at about 2348.

The most likely source of the torpedoes was *Oyashio*, which had fired at the blazing "battleship" (*Pensacola*) ten minutes before. The torpedoes missed *Pensacola* but continued on to nail the unseen *Northampton*—*Oyashio* claimed three hits out of eight torpedoes. *Kuroshio* fired a spread of four torpedoes at 2345 at an "enemy battleship," but they were less than halfway there when *Northampton* was hit. At 2352, *Kagero* reported firing four torpedoes at the enemy "battleship" and lashing her with gunfire, but at this time both *Pensacola* and *Northampton* were afire and neither reported additional hits—both crews were undoubtedly so busy fighting their raging fires that they would have been unlikely to notice a destroyer in the shadows. Almost an hour later, when *Oyashio* and *Kuroshio* were sent back to help *Takanami*, the latter fired her last two torpedoes at the enemy "battleship," presumably *Northampton*, with no apparent results.

Figure 6. *Positions at 2325 and U.S. gunfire between 2320 and 2325.*

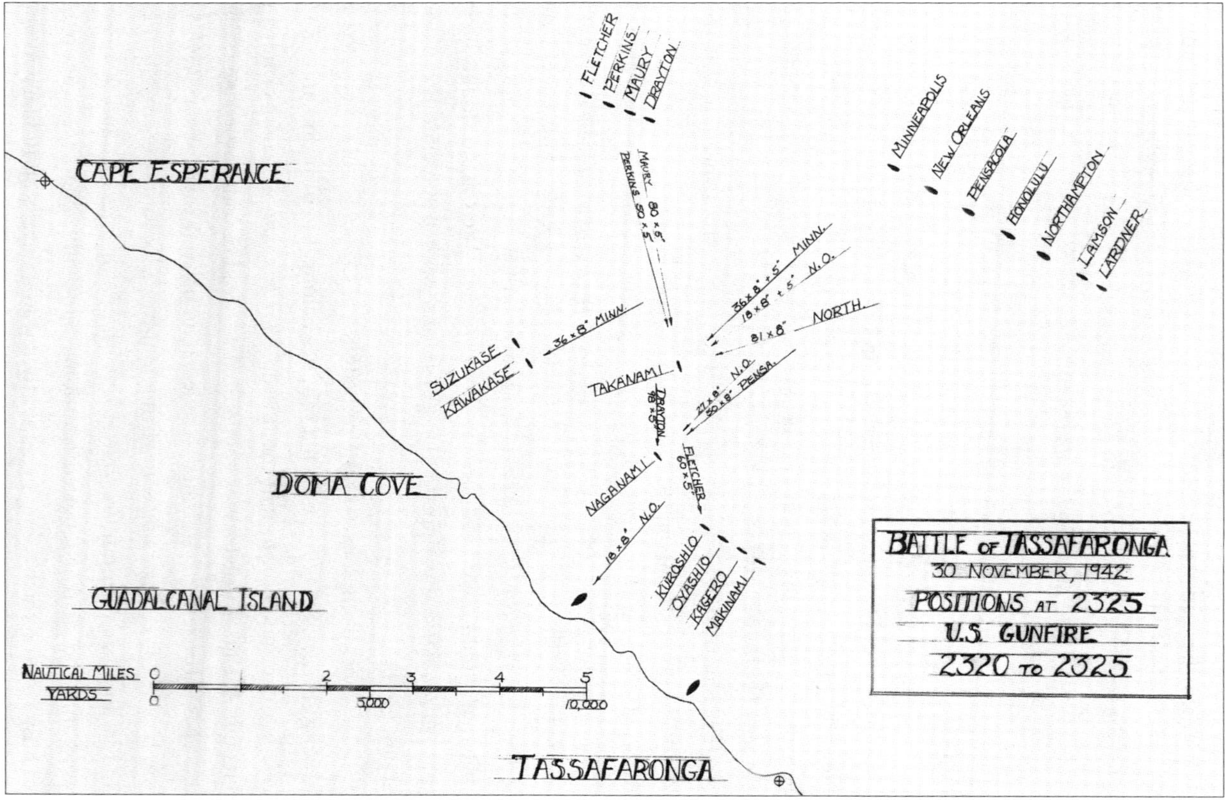

Figure 7. *Positions at 2330 with gun and torpedo fire between 2325 and 2330.*

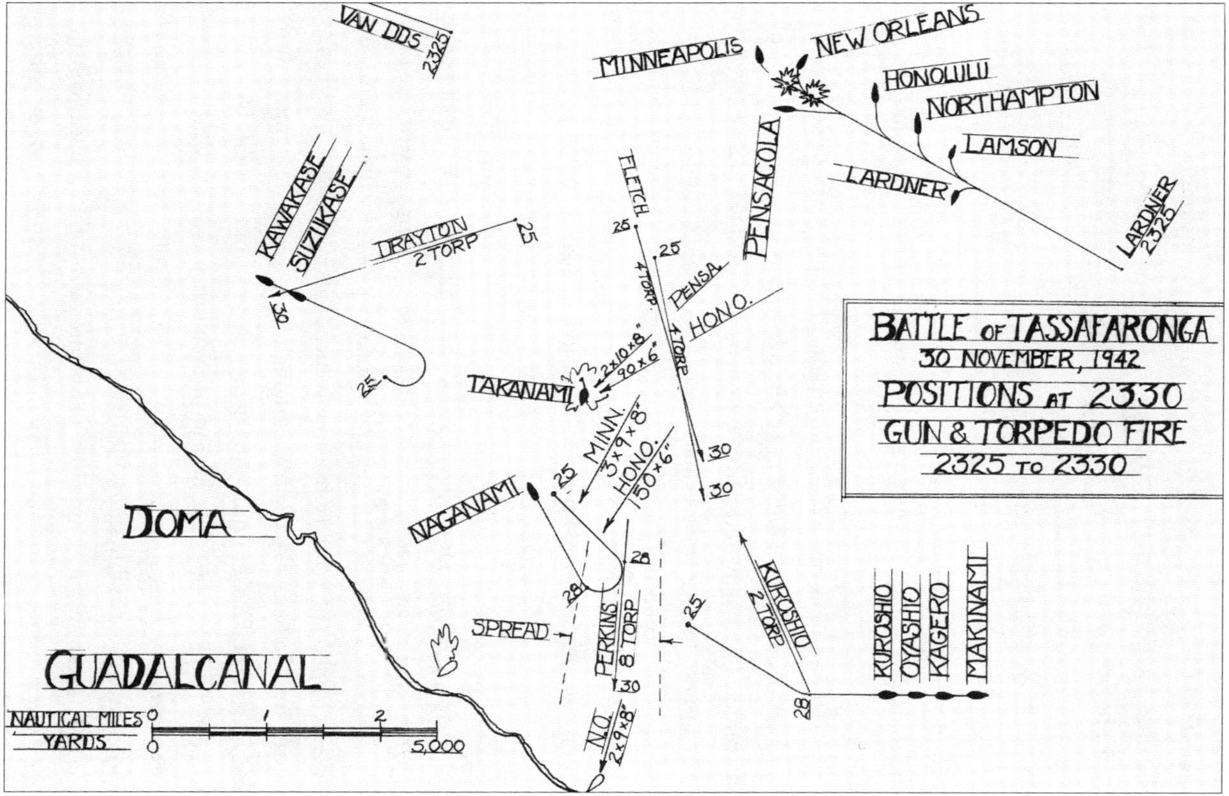

BATTLE of TASSAFARONGA
30 NOVEMBER, 1942
POSITIONS at 2330
GUN & TORPEDO FIRE
2325 TO 2330

MAKINAMI
KAGERO
OYASHIO
KUROSHIO

LARDNER 2325
NORTHAMPTON
LAMSON
HONOLULU
LARDNER
NEW ORLEANS
MINNEAPOLIS
PENSACOLA
FLETCH
HONO.
PENSA.
25
25
30
30
4 TORP.
4 TORP.
KUROSHIO
2 TORP
28

MINN.
5×9×8"
HONO.
150×6"
3×20×8"
TAKANAMI
25
NAGANAMI
PERKINS
8 TORP
N.O.
2×4×8"
SPREAD
24
28
30
VAN DUS. 2325
DRAYTON
2 TORP
25
KAWAKASE
SUZUKASE
30

DOMA
GUADALCANAL

NAUTICAL MILES
0   1   2
YARDS
0   5,000

The last American blow at the enemy was *Drayton*'s half-salvo of low-speed torpedoes, fired at 2338. Though it was shrugged off in Wright's report and drew sharp criticism from Halsey as a waste of ammunition, it was, in fact a valid shot. *Drayton*'s target was *Naganami,* which was making at least 36 knots at the time and perhaps more as Tanaka reported. Although they probably missed astern because of the extremely high speed of the target, the torpedo run of just over 11,000 yards was within the capability of the Mk-15 at the speed setting—*Drayton*'s crew reported explosions as the torpedoes hit the reefs after crossing the target's track, proving they got that far. It seems to the author to be a distortion of values to criticize a captain for firing his available weapons and taking the chance they will hit when his ship is already at risk and he has the enemy in his sights.

Why *Honolulu* contributed so little to the action after she sheered northward out of column can only be explained by failure of her SG. These wonderful instruments were new to the fleet and many bugs had yet to be worked out. The early installations were particularly disturbed by shock and vibration and their effectiveness declined as the disturbance continued. The intense vibration during the three sessions of continuous fire would certainly have put any installation to test. Although all seven of the surviving Japanese destroyers were within 15,000 yards of *Honolulu* at 2340 as she prepared to pass close to Savo Island, she detected none of them. Later, when she made her last sweep of Iron Bottom Bay before clearing out to the west for the night, she failed to detect the two Japanese destroyers that had been sent back to stand by the stricken *Takanami*.

The same can be said of Admiral Tisdale, who was catapulted into command by the crippling of Wright's flagship. Depending on *Honolulu*'s weakened radar, he saw little so he could do little. Although his inquiries were timely, he did not feel he could take over until he finally got orders from Wright. He was ordered to take charge at 0001, but he had little information with which to work. He directed *Honolulu* in a fruitless sweep to the north of Savo and made an effort to gather the still operable ships. Neither *Honolulu*'s SG radar nor TBS was up to the task, and it was an hour and a half before he had things under control.

Which brings us to *Lamson* and *Lardner* and the almost forgotten Commander Abercrombie, ComDesDiv 9. With no instructions otherwise, *Lamson* tried to help by firing star shells for the first 10 minutes of the battle. Her efforts were not helpful to either her friends or to her enemies. Those star shells falling to the right of her line of sight to *Takanami,* which would have been about half of those she fired, were blinding to the lead destroyers, and all of them were blinding to the Japanese. They probably also helped draw attention away from Sato's four ships as they sped to the southeast and they certainly laid down a wall of brilliant flares between the American gunners and the ships off Doma Cove. That Abercrombie led his ships to the east and clear of the battle after they were taken under fire by the heavy machine-gun batteries of the American cruisers can only be described as prudent. No one had given him any orders at all.

The one remaining mystery of this confusing night is the matter of the capsized destroyer *Minneapolis* reported almost ramming and eventually passing close aboard. The narrative of the action report, which was probably all that Admiral Wright considered in his evaluation, implies this wreckage was sighted about 0215, after *Minneapolis* had changed course to head for Tulagi. Her track chart, obviously a rough reconstruction made up from the quartermaster's notebook, however, records the wreckage was passed close aboard at 2349, shortly after she changed course to head for Lunga Point. Captain Rosendahl reported, "This derelict was unmistakably a destroyer bow with a lengthy section of other structure attached to it," and Wright's list of information items reported, "Visible part of keel variously estimated as 300 to 500 feet." You guessed it—the plot shows *Minneapolis* was passing close to *New Orleans'* severed bow.

The SOC pilots flying over the battle area should have been the most valuable source of information of all to Admiral Wright in trying to figure out what had happened, because they had a bird's-eye view of the action. He referred to their observations in his summary list of information at the beginning of his report, but the well-meaning aviators were actually more misleading than helpful. Enclosure (C) of the *Minneapolis* action report is entitled, "Information Furnished by *Minneapolis* Aviators," and contains the information reported by Lieutenant L. L. Booda and Lieutenant (jg) R. J. Hauge. The pertinent paragraphs are quoted, accompanied by the author's comment, as follows:

3. Soon after our cruisers opened fire, the aviators observed at least 3 heavy ships, undoubtedly Jap transports, on fire off Tassafaronga, and very quickly these burning ships disappeared, presumably by sinking. The aviators saw a total of 5 and possibly 6 ships in the transport area, and are positive that the Jap transports were too far off the beach to have landed anything.

Comment: These were the beached transports fired at by *New Orleans*. A total of five beached wrecks in the vicinity of Tassafaronga are shown in today's charts.

4.   At about the time the *Minneapolis* was torpedoed, the aviators observed enemy ships firing towards the *Minneapolis*. These enemy ships were forward of the port beam of the *Minneapolis* and well to the northward of the Jap transport area. The aviators are positive that these enemy ships were between the Jap transport area and our own battle lines.

Comment: *Takanami* and *Naganami* and perhaps some of Sato's ships were then firing at our cruisers.

5.   While proceeding to the shore line of Guadalcanal, these aviators saw a column of 6 DDs, judged to be destroyers from their high speed and their size, heading easterly close in to the shore line, and definitely between the shore line and the wall of star shell illumination being set up in the Jap transport area. (They have surmised that there may have been more than 6 vessels but they definitely saw the 6 DDs). This was just about the time that the main firing of our force had been completed or was dwindling. When the planes were a little better than half way between Cape Esperance and Lunga Point, the planes passed over the six DDs, and as they did the column of Jap DDs made a sharp left 180 degree turn, and proceeded westerly at high speed, still between the coast line and the star shell illumination; the turning point of the column was beyond the east end of the illumination.

Comment: Sato's four ships plus *Takanami* and *Naganami* would account for the report of six ships—they were the only ones underway at the beginning. The sharp turn about the time the cruiser firing dwindled would correspond to Sato's four ships, but the Japanese reported turning to the right.

7.   On their first trip from Cape Esperance to Savo Island, the aviators observed a heavy ship on course 270°, proceeding at an estimated speed of 30 knots. This ship appeared to be undamaged and was a very long ship, in their opinion possibly a heavy cruiser and definitely not one of our own. As far as the aviators know, this vessel escaped undamaged.

Comment: This plots as *Naganami.*

8. On the second trip of the planes from Cape Esperance to Savo Island, the aviators observed a heavy ship, smoking badly, proceeding westward at slow speed. The aviators judged this to be an enemy ship of the same size as the one reported in the preceding paragraph proceeding westward at high speed. The aviators believe that neither of these two ships proceeding westerly, from their point of view of them, could have been an American ship. The smoking ship was about half way between Savo Island and Cape Esperance when sighted. When last seen by our aviators this ship was still steaming westward and smoking.

Comment: This corresponds to the damaged *Pensacola.*

10. The aviators state that on leaving Esperance toward Savo Island the second time, they observed a tremendous explosion of a large ship, the ball of flame from which extended over 2,000 feet into the air. The position of this exploding ship is reported as about two miles east of the middle of Savo Island. Lieutenant Booda is of the opinion that the violence of the explosion indicated ammunition rather than fuel oil or gasoline, suggesting that it might have been an ammunition ship.

Comment: This was *Northampton.*

Obviously the view from above was not much more accurate than that below—the aviators too were expecting to see transports and they saw them.

But this analysis would not be complete without commenting on the blinding effect of smokeless powder. Although the American torpedoes had failed to do their job, both the gunners at the scene and the admirals reviewing the reports felt confident that the cruisers' guns could and would redress the balance. All reports praised the volume and accuracy of the 8-inch batteries and words were hardly adequate to express the appreciation of *Honolulu*'s 6-inch gunnery. The only problem was that the force's eyesight and optics were paralyzed by the blinding flashes from the guns and dazzled by the star shell glare, so that the directors could not be kept on target and observation of the results were faulty. The accuracy and effectiveness of the American gun batteries were incredibly bad and the observers on the spot were too blinded by gun flashes and stars in their eyes to see it.

All commanders spoke of need for flashless powder and Washington was working on the problem, but the needed powder was not on hand on the 30th of November. This battle was a monument to the limited view of those naval officers who, remembering Jutland and Dogger Bank, imagined that all important battles would be fought in daylight. The Japanese high command had invested heavily in the ability to fight at night, and they collected their dividends at Tassafaronga.

⸺ XII ⸺
EPILOG

It has given the author great personal satisfaction to learn what really happened on that fateful night in Iron Bottom Bay more than fifty years ago. It was fascinating for the author to read the reports from both sides of the conflict and feel he was in touch with the best possible sources of information. He hopes his effort will be appreciated as a contribution to naval history, but he could not leave this fascinating battle without making some additional personal observations.

The contrast between the two on-scene commanders, Wright and Tanaka, is striking. They were both career naval officers well qualified and well prepared for their tasks. Tanaka was in his tenth year of Japan's long national war of expansion and had been commanding Destroyer Squadron Two at the forefront of the war with America since it began. He had as much combat experience as any man still alive, and he had been at the center of the Solomons struggle for three hectic months. He was a destroyer officer through and through and he believed in his wonderful weapon, the Type 93 torpedo, and the skill of his men to use it. He gave only two orders, in effect, "Get ready" and "Go."

Wright's destroyer experience reached back to World War I, and in the late 1930s he had commanded a heavy cruiser before being promoted to command a division of them. Although he had commanded TF-67 for only two days, he was as thoroughly prepared for the task as 30 years of naval service could make him. Over the years he had participated in every type of fleet maneuver by day or night and every type of gunnery or torpedo exercise that existed. Every commander under him was a regular naval officer, trained in the same school and to the same standard. They all used the same signal book and knew the fleet maneuvers and tactics by heart. As normal in the U.S. Fleet organization and operations, any ship was instantly ready to respond to any tactical order. The fact that his force was hastily assembled, with the exception of *Lamson* and *Lardner,* which arrived too late to receive Wright's instructions about star shells, had no bearing on the outcome. Even the belabored fact that the lead destroyers lacked a division commander was not a factor; Cole did an outstanding job of handling the ships under his command.

Wright was heavily burdened by the previous battles. The catastrophe of the first Savo haunted his planning and he could not forget that of his predecessors in the three previous battles, only Lee was still alive. He followed Kinkaid's lead and filled in the details. As his ships entered Iron Bottom Bay and swept westward in a long quarter echelon, he had set the stage perfectly. When the long fingers of his radars found the enemy, his first move to turn right and bring his ships into a column was good, but he would have done better to maintain his original line of bearing and continue to maneuver by simultaneous turns as he had said he would. His first order, which restrained the lead destroyers from firing when their leader thought best, was a mistake, but boring in to shorter range and ordering his ships to open fire with guns before the torpedoes had a chance to reach their targets was a worse mistake. He was basically a one-weapon warrior, whose concentration was centered on the big guns of his cruisers.

Nevertheless, Carleton Wright handled his battle with every bit as much skill as shown during the best moments of Lee, Callahan, or Scott. The American admirals did not maneuver their ships with confidence and skill in the dark, although it is hard to understand why, since the ships under their command performed intricate maneuvers every night in normal task force cruising. They also concentrated more on controlling the weapons of their ships than they did on placing the ships into positions where those weapons could be most effectively used—a habit that interfered with the efficient use of both guns and torpedoes in all of the Savo battles except Lee's. They were excellent planners and good strategists, but when they came into contact with the enemy, they appeared to freeze. Once the engagement started they seemed to forget they could change course and speed to confound the enemy and cause his weapons to miss.

It was not the ships and crews which most needed the training as implied by Nimitz, it was the admirals. In actual battle they were called upon to think and act in real time, without delay. They needed to know their ships and their weapons thoroughly—particularly the newest features like the SG and FC radars—and they needed to know both their capabilities and limitations. They needed to practice with their instruments of war enough to feel comfortable about using them. They needed to trust their subordinates and be ready to tell them, "Go to it"—to do that for which they were trained.

Admiral Halsey's sharp criticism of Commander Cole in paragraph 4 of his endorsement is regrettable. Cole had maneuvered his ships with skill and determination, would have made a nearly perfect torpedo attack except for the interference of Admiral Wright, engaged the enemy with guns until he had no more targets, then disengaged and cleared as instructed. He led his ships around Savo at near-maximum speed, then deployed them appropriately and headed south to re-engage. For this a cloud of disapproval descended upon him, while Admiral Tisdale in *Honolulu,* following in Cole's wake, disappeared to the north and didn't come back to Iron Bottom Bay until almost 0100. Halsey found Tisdale's actions commendable and said he demonstrated "superior qualities of initiative and leadership." Halsey, joining the ranks of one-weapon commanders, thought of destroyers as small ships supplied to assist larger ships, not as major warships in their own right. He obviously didn't realize that he was commenting on a battle which had dramatically demonstrated that, at night, poorly handled cruisers were no match for well-handled destroyers equipped with good torpedoes.

The lack of accurate knowledge of the existence and capability of the Type 93 torpedo was not the fault of anyone in Task Force Sixty-Seven. Why Naval Intelligence had not learned about it is not known. Certainly the world was aware that Japan was constructing new destroyers with exceptionally large torpedo mounts. There was even a joke going around that the Japanese destroyers were so top-heavy from their heavy armament that at least one of them had capsized. But even a neophyte should have wondered about the armament, particularly why the torpedoes and their heavy mounts were so large.

What was the Navy Department doing to find out what was going on? The simplest photographs would have revealed the size of the weapons and their prominent placement on the ships. CinCPac, CNO, and BuOrd should all have been dazzled by the Japanese torpedoes at Pearl Harbor—at least to impress them that the Japanese had excellent torpedoes. It was admittedly difficult to quantify the performance of the Japanese torpedoes during the melees of mid-November, but no room was left for doubt about their lethality as ship after ship was mortally wounded. Etched more clearly the previous August, *Quincy* and *Vincennes* had been gutted by Japanese torpedoes and sank within an hour. ComSoPac or CinCPac should have concluded that Japanese torpedoes were unexpectedly lethal and cautioned their commanders to stay well out of torpedo range and use their guns at the long ranges for which they were designed.

An underlying cause for this failure to perceive the obvious was a deep belief that everything American was the best and everything foreign was inferior. This may be good medicine for propagandists, but it is a poor way to prepare for war. The Japanese were so interested in what was going on outside their small country that every Japanese traveler came to be considered a camera-toting spy. The Japanese military had been planning the Greater East Asia War for 40 years and they were completely ready to buy or, if necessary, steal any technical development that might benefit them. The U.S. Navy was sure that its big guns, highly developed armor, wonderful smokeless powder, incomparable fire control equipment, and even the Mk-15 torpedo, with its devastating Mk-6 exploder, were the best in the world. Since being given credit for saving the world for democracy at the end of World War I, the American psyche was infected with a paralyzing self-satisfaction that stifled inquiry and criticism. If only the American torpedoes had been realistically tested and their faults corrected before Pearl Harbor, the entire history of the first two years of World War II would have been different. American submarines would have become devastating to Japanese plans by the middle of 1942, not two years later. Coral Sea, Midway, Stewart Island, Santa Cruz, anywhere aerial torpedoes could have been used would have had more favorable outcomes, and the vicious night engagements in Iron Bottom Bay would have left a lot more Japanese wreckage on the bottom. The entire Solomons campaign and those that followed would have been shorter and less costly.

Imagine what would have happened if our battleships had not been crippled at Pearl Harbor and Admiral Yamamoto had succeeded in drawing the American Battle Line into a major fleet engagement as he had planned. Vice Admiral William S. Pye, Commander Battle Force, in classic fashion as had been rehearsed repeatedly during fleet exercises immediately before the war, would have maneuvered to bring the two great fleets together with the columns of battleships steaming on roughly parallel courses, twenty to thirty thousand yards apart, flanked by divisions of cruisers, thrust forward toward the enemy, both fore and aft, and with the destroyer flotillas deployed ahead and behind them, torpedoes ready. As the heavy guns spoke in measured cadence, the American destroyer squadrons would bore in, guns blazing, taking heavy losses as they fought in to killing range, to fire massive fans of crisscrossing torpedoes to decimate the enemy battleships. Symmetrically the Japanese light forces, both destroyer and cruiser, would approach, but not close enough to alarm the American commander. Their torpedoes would probably enter the water unseen. Taking fewer losses, the enemy wings would surprise the Americans by falling back. With minor exceptions, the American torpedoes would pass harmlessly under the keels of the Japanese battle line, and its big guns would continue to pound away. The massive waves of Japanese torpedoes, to the contrary, would have dotted the American formation with towering explosions, shattering hulls and spreading devastation. The results of such a battle could have been far more damaging to the fleet and to the morale of the American people than the perfidy of Pearl Harbor. It is one thing to be caught unprepared in peacetime—quite another to be beaten in a fair fight.

The Japanese Type 93 torpedo was as great a step forward in naval warfare as the German V-2 was in land warfare. It introduced new dimensions for a class of weapons, moving them up the scale from commonplace to critical. The idea was not so unusual, in fact both the British and the Germans also had submarine torpedoes running on oxygen before the end of the war. It was the concept of a "Super Torpedo" with unheard-of range, speed, and striking power, plus the courage and imagination of the naval leadership that shaped a fleet and a strategic policy around it, that made the Type 93 so dangerous. It took technical cleverness, large investments, and dogged determination to bring it to reality. The Japanese did it. The American Navy, believing in its own superiority and blindly hiding its mistakes behind curtains of secrecy, did not.

We have come a long way since the Depression days of the 1930s and we have come a long way from the chauvinism of the small band of experts who guided the Navy's weapon development in the preceding years. Our country spends more each year on weapons research and development than it did on the entire Navy before the war. We have vast establishments devoted to test and evaluation just to ensure that devices such as the Mk-6 exploders can't enter service unless they perform as advertised. So, though this may be a bit of interesting history, could shortcomings such as those that led to the unbelievable events off Tassafaronga go undetected again?

As long as an elite group is permitted to corner the market of a particular area of information, as long as specific designs can be shielded from scrutiny by the label of "secret," as long as any weapon is not fully tested against real targets under realistic conditions, watch out. Warheads and fuzes are the critical elements of damaging the enemy; have they been tested against actual targets? Did they destroy the incoming missile, sink the ship, knock out the bridge support? Detectors and trackers are critical; do they work in all weather, when the ship is firing or being hit, can they be blinded, or worse, misled? Computers are so capable they can do almost anything, whether it needs to be done or not. Are our command and communications systems serving the commander in the field, or the software gurus and scorekeepers at home? Are the designers, industrialists, government laboratories, systems analysts, military staffs, politicians, and bureaucrats helping the warrior, or standing between him and his weapons?

Failures such as the unsuspected shortcomings of the Mk-6 and the Mk-15 could still go undetected today when anything less than absolute reality is permitted in the testing. To determine whether an anti-submarine torpedo is effective, it has to be tested against real submarines or an authentic equivalent, unless one wishes to risk repeating the Mk-6 experience. To determine whether an anti-ship missile is lethal, it must be fired against real ships and the damage evaluated—a ship with a damaged superstructure is not destroyed and it may return to fight again. Guns and guided missiles must be fired against multiple targets at realistic speeds and altitudes, and in realistically adverse weather. Designs and development must be exposed to the scrutiny of qualified outside experts, who don't have a vested interest in the success of the project or in the acceptance of the product.

Equally important is to ensure that our military intelligence establishment is in fact contributing to the knowledge of our military leaders. Vast amounts of data stored in secret vaults are useless unless the critical facts reach the mind of the official who needs them. The designer of the missile seeker or fuze needs to know what countermeasures his enemy might realistically possess and use, not what is technically possible. The radar designer needs to know what are the characteristics of his real target, not a scientist's guess at what is achievable with unlimited expenditure. The problem with intelligence is not so much its gathering, although that may well be difficult—it is the evaluation of that which is gathered. Only by breaking down the stultifying walls of secrecy can the valuable information be filtered from the masses of chaff and put at the service of those who can use it. And the gatherer and the analyst have no way of knowing which individuals on the ships, in the squadrons, on the staffs, in the laboratories, and in industry need the information. Who knows who has a "need to know" when a new weapon is being invented?

It is hoped that the analysis of this battle has helped clarify the events which were reported and has rectified some of the misjudgments previously made. Most of all, it is hoped that it will stimulate the reader to examine current weapons and equipment to make sure that our military forces have the best and most reliable weapons in the world. We may have the most capable young people in the world, but if we don't give them effective and reliable weapons, they won't produce victory when the nation needs it.

Index _

About the Author

Russell Sydnor Crenshaw Jr., Captain, USN (Ret.), graduated from the Naval Academy in 1941. As gunnery and executive officer of USS *Maury* (DD-401) during 1941–43, he participated in many key engagements during the Solomon Islands campaign, including the Battle of Tassafaronga in 1942 and the Battles of Kolombangara and Vella Gulf in 1943, as described in his book, *South Pacific Destroyer.* Later in World War II he served as executive officer of USS *Stormes* (DD-780). Postwar, he commanded USS *Cogswell* (DD-651) and placed into commission USS *Forrest Sherman* (DD-931). Later, he helped introduce guided missiles to the Navy's arsenal. Following his retirement from the Navy, he worked for several companies as a consultant for weapons systems. He is the author of the classic professional text *Naval Shiphandling* and lives in Drayden, Md.